What Your Colleagues Are Saying . . .

We've all seen good ideas, programs, and initiatives fail. What if the problem was not the program, but our skill in dealing with the crises that occurred as the program was implemented? I wish I had had this book years ago to learn the skills necessary to address the realities and challenges of implementation.

—**Douglas Fisher**, Professor,
San Diego State University,
San Diego, California

Jim Marshall's extensive experience and deep wisdom take the lead in this powerful book. With helpful research and theory Marshall has created a singular handbook that leads us to the clear analysis and practical action steps we need in those sometimes shaky, critical mid-initiative or mid-project moments that we all experience.

—**Peggy O'Brien**, Director of Education,
Folger Shakespeare Library,
Washington, DC

Educational leaders have the benefit and the burden of leading change that will positively impact our scholars. Fortunately, Dr. Jim Marshall provides the foundational concepts we need to boldly tackle the multi-faceted demands of our work. Creatively written in a how-to format, this is a must-add to the school leaders' toolbox. It will revolutionize your practice and transform your organizational outcomes.

—**Helen V. Griffith**, Superintendent,
The Preuss School UC San Diego,
La Jolla, California

Marshall offers a refreshing perspective born from real-world experiences. This book isn't just for those in crisis mode; it's a guide for all educational leaders seeking to understand, anticipate, and mitigate the challenges inherent in any initiative. Emphasizing the power of leveraging strengths amidst challenges, Marshall provides a practical and valuable roadmap for overcoming obstacles and achieving impact.

—**Jamie Annunzio Myers**, Chief Operating Officer &
Senior Vice President, Education and Engagement,
PBS SoCal,
Los Angeles, California

When it comes to school initiatives there is no lack of good ideas. What is lacking is quality implementation. Too often we don't realize this until we're well into the program and not getting the results we expected. If that's your situation, this is the book for you. Jim Marshall tells you what to do when implementation isn't working, so you can quickly turn things around and achieve the positive impact you seek.

—**Jim Knight**, Author, *Instructional Coaching: A Partnership Approach to Improving Instruction*, Co-Founder, Instructional Coaching Group, North Loup, Nebraska

Working in education is complex and often unpredictable. When surprises happen and things go awry, Jim Marshall's practical guidance provides a path forward. With it, you'll be able to navigate from a position of strength, not defense, leveraging your data and expertise with confidence.

—**Laura G. Hunter**, Chief Operating Officer & KUEN Station Manager, Utah Education Network, Salt Lake City, Utah

Fixing Education Initiatives in Crisis is a powerful guide for anyone seeking practical solutions to the challenges facing education today. Dr. Marshall's wealth of experience shines through as he provides actionable tools to tackle complex problems. His strategic approach, grounded in measurable outcomes, is a beacon for leaders navigating the ever-evolving educational landscape to drive meaningful change and foster student success.

—**Sean Hauze**, Senior Director, Instructional Technology Services, San Diego State University, San Diego, California

Fixing Education Initiatives in Crisis

24 Go-to Strategies

James Marshall

Foreword by Jody Spiro

For information:

Corwin
A Sage Company
2455 Teller Road
Thousand Oaks, California 91320
(800) 233-9936
www.corwin.com

Sage Publications Ltd.
1 Oliver's Yard
55 City Road
London EC1Y 1SP
United Kingdom

Sage Publications India Pvt. Ltd.
Unit No 323-333, Third Floor, F-Block
International Trade Tower Nehru Place
New Delhi 110 019
India

Sage Publications Asia-Pacific Pte. Ltd.
18 Cross Street #10-10/11/12
China Square Central
Singapore 048423

Printed in the United States of America

Paperback ISBN 978-1-0719-4244-4

This book is printed on acid-free paper.

Vice President and Editorial Director: Monica Eckman
Senior Acquisitions Editor: Tanya Ghans
Content Development Manager: Desirée A. Bartlett
Senior Editorial Assistant: Nyle De Leon
Production Editor: Vijayakumar
Copy Editor: Colleen Brennan
Typesetter: TNQ Tech Pvt. Ltd.
Proofreader: Girish Sharma
Indexer: TNQ Tech Pvt. Ltd.
Cover Designer: Scott Van Atta
Marketing Manager: Melissa Duclos

24 25 26 27 28 10 9 8 7 6 5 4 3 2 1

Contents

List of Figures

List of Tables

List of Strategies

Foreword

James Marshall has given us an important set of resources to help leaders and teams bring desired change into reality. It provides insights and tools grounded by the very nature of the dynamics of change.

Ironically, "change" is the only constant in leadership, as the recent COVID crisis has shown. As leaders, you and your teams need to base your strategies on the notion that the work is ever evolving. The idea is to harness that dynamic and use it to best advantage when moving forward. Effective change is based on clarity of vision and goals and, even then, you cannot guarantee the outcome.

Therefore, it is of great value that initiatives be led by teams, so multiple perspectives can be engaged. Teams need to resist relying on "we do it this way because that's the way we have always done things" and plan for the disruption of the status quo and for the tendency to revert to the status quo once the crisis is over.

The idea is to catch problems early and use them to make improvements. For these reasons, those who effectively lead change understand that the initial plan must be carefully and regularly monitored according to milestones. We must change how we think about "plans." They are not to be developed and then left to gather dust on the shelf. They need to be living documents that are revised as the experience and learning requires.

Which leads us to the main premise of this book, "Never let a good crisis go to waste." Instead of dreading crises, learn how to anticipate them and use them as a source for learning and continuous improvement.

Above all, effective change requires teams to be intentional. The 24 tools in this book will support you in making deliberate use of crises to lead change strategies effectively toward your team's important vision and goals. These tools are based on evidence and experience. They are not prescriptive but are adaptable by you for your context. Whether you need to increase support for your program or identify a missing perspective, this book will serve you well on your continuous journey for high impact initiatives. I wish you much success as you pursue your important work.

—**Jody Spiro**
Author *Leading Change Step-by-Step: Tactics, Tools, and Tales*
Strategic Advisor, Learning Forward

Preface

Stacie Alexander (2023), a colleague and former doctoral student at my university, conducted a brilliant needs assessment for her dissertation. In it, she examined the unique needs of students with adverse childhood experiences (ACEs) as they reflected upon their experiences immediately following their high school graduation. With a deep and data-rich understanding, she was able to recommend detailed changes in, and enhancements to, her district's programs and supports for these important students. Inquiry, thought, and understanding preceded action. Further, the process she followed is a metaphorical prophylactic that directly counters the chances of a program reaching the point of crisis.

Summarizing her adventure with needs assessment, she offered a familiar analogy applied in a unique way. When it comes to programs in schools and across districts, she observed that we typically put lots of eggs in a single basket. We hope some will hatch. And we wait around to see which ones—if any—do. After a period of time—often too short of an "incubation" period—we launch into lengthy discussions about why most didn't hatch. Often, those discussions happen in the absence of concrete, objective data to understand the causes and implications, truly and factually. Inevitably, having gone to the trouble of placing the egg in the basket, the lack of a full hatch results in some level of crisis, the need for intervention, and even herculean efforts to "save" an egg that may never have had a chance of fully hatching, let alone thriving. We spend days, weeks, months, and even years, trying to "make" programs happen, sometimes with success, sometimes without, but almost always with a level of effort far greater than need be.

Alexander's post-dissertation epiphanies were these: Needs assessment is a valuable, necessary process that must lead any press to create a new program. It's agnostic to content; it can be applied anywhere, with anyone, and with anything. From her accomplished vantage point, needs assessment overturns the basket of eggs by allowing us to pick the "right" ones. We end up with fewer eggs, but they are the ones that are most likely to thrive in the context of our challenge. If one can purposely preselect from a dozen eggs the ones that will predictably hatch into chicks, isn't it worth the up-front investment?

This book is about programs in crisis. There are many reasons why programs and initiatives boil over. But Alexander's observations are relevant to each one. Violating the basic processes of understanding before undertaking, inquiry before ideation, and reflection before reaction are predictable ways to summon a crisis. As you read, understand, and formulate solutions to the crises you face, know that it is never too late for a bit of inquiry dedicated to understanding a situation or opportunity with **fresh eyes**.

So, here's to embracing the crisis, or crises, you face. Come to know it, understand it, and appreciate it for the opportunity it is. In that way, you'll resist quick fixes and stop-gap measures while investing in lasting solutions that not only allow your program to thrive but also to return predictable, meaningful results.

Acknowledgments

I'm grateful for every adventure with learning programs and initiatives. From implementing those designed by others, to many of my own design, there is no shortage of learning that happens when "program meets world." They change lives. There isn't one among us who cannot think back to a formative education program experience that shaped who we are today. Having evaluated hundreds of funded education programs and products, I continue to learn from amazing educators, sharp educational leaders, and university colleagues who, every day, surface new ideas and innovations.

I want to acknowledge the people, of late, who have supported me in these endeavors, which generate many of the insights that are central to this book.

So, I first credit my esteemed friends and colleagues Doug Fisher and Nancy Frey. Their support, collaboration, and cheerleading of my work propels me forward daily. Our latest work in the Republic of Georgia with early childhood programs has delivered another life-changing opportunity to evolve our understanding of initiative best practice while serving an amazing country and contributing to a more prosperous path for its youngest learners. For that project, in particular, I'm grateful to Tamar Tchkonia, Georgia Innovation, Inclusion, and Quality (I2Q) Project ECE Component Lead, and Tamar Sanikidze, Georgia I2Q Project Executive Director, two amazing educational leaders within the Ministry of Education who are doing much to effect positive change across Georgia's entire education system.

I've also been fortunate to work with, and learn from, some of the best minds in environmental education, including the U.S. Fish and Wildlife Service SoCal Urban Refuge Wildlife Project team leaders: Chantel Jiminez, Andy Yuen, and Jill Terp. The work extends to more than 20 community program partners who are implementing diverse environmental and STEM-focused programming across the entire Southern California region. We've learned much, including a traditionally outdoor program's ability to pivot to technology delivery once COVID sidelined face-to-face learning. For these smart and strategic thinkers, I'm especially thankful.

I want to acknowledge three colleagues who have each provided examples that illustrate the application of various strategies throughout this book. My gratitude to Laura Hunter of the Utah Education Network, Rachel Miller of San Diego Unified School District, and James Garrison of Escondido Union School District.

Three former graduate students, now successful and valued colleagues, continue to influence my thinking. Sean Hauze, Joaquin Ortiz, and Matthew Wilson shared their minds, helpful critiques, and perspectives toward the realization of this book. In particular, I'm thankful for Matt's intuitive approach to creating visuals that convey concepts in places where words fall short. Their collective wisdom is evidenced on the pages you'll soon read, and my own ideas are only made better by their insights.

I'm grateful to Sarah Milo Hoskow and Rachel Strang, leaders with inquirED. They helpfully reviewed the early ideas for this book and offered their feedback and insight, while being transparent with the flavors of challenges they face when implementing programs. Their vivid ground truth also resides in the pages that follow.

I remain indebted to the clients and colleagues with whom I've had the privilege to engage and support over more than 20 years in the education field. Many are named and featured in this book as a result of their successful initiative efforts. Too many to name individually, my gratitude extends to the school districts across the country, non-profits—especially public media, museums and libraries, and the funded program work that has been supported by the National Science Foundation, National Endowment for the Humanities, U.S. Department of Education, many state departments of education, county offices of education, and international agencies, and the list could go on.

Finally, there once again would be no book without the friends and family I'm fortunate to have in my life.

- Top of this list is Senior Editor Tanya Ghans. Her insight is limitless, her belief in our projects, unwavering. I'm fortunate to continue our collaboration while benefitting every day from her insight, intuition, and innovation.

- To Steve, Ian, and Luc for encouragement in words, laughs, pie, and the protected writing space that is the Woodlands muse.

- To Sarah, Richard, Griffin, and London for the requisite reflection time that makes ideas grow.

- To Debbie and Lou for positive words, encouragement, and a belief in the outcome sometimes even I seem to forget.

- Finally, to Kevin, Nick, Joe, and Evan, for seeing me through one of the most vivid, program-related crises of my adult life, one from which I gained enormous amounts of clarity around both crisis and leadership. The results are delivered as wisdom on the pages that follow.

About the Author

James Marshall's life-long work lies at the intersection of people and the organizations in which they work and optimizing the synergy that fertile convergence holds. His scholarship, teaching, and consulting combine our understanding of human performance and organization development to assess strengths, devise strategy, and improve even the most vexing of challenges. Engagements have found him doing everything from evaluating virtual reality–delivered training for active shooter containment, to devising strategy that improved the community-focused impacts realized by the national network of over 150 public television stations.

He is currently Professor of Educational Leadership at San Diego State University, in the #1 ranked California State University College of Education. In his private practice, he serves as a thought partner to leaders seeking to hasten the collective impact of their organization's investments, especially their human resources. From assessing strengths and needs, to conceptualizing strategy and initiatives, and then measuring return on investment, Dr. Marshall's unique approach relies on a proven mix of assessment and evaluation, appreciative inquiry, and empathic understanding that predictably yields quantifiable results. Clients particularly note his ability to use data—with novelty and persuasion—to drive change.

With over 200 publications to his credit, Dr. Marshall's scholarship encompasses a diverse range of works that include empirical research, program evaluation efforts, and policy development. His program evaluation endeavors are particularly significant and include over 250 individual studies of funded projects and program investments totaling more than $150 million. This work has been funded by diverse agencies that include the National Science Foundation, the National Endowment for the Humanities, the Institute for Library and Museum Services, the Public Broadcasting Service, and the Corporation for Public Broadcasting, as well as the U.S. Department of Education, U.S. Department of Health and Human Services, U.S. Department of the Interior, and the Transportation Security Administration. His work with state and local education agencies, school systems, and regional offices of education encompasses 40 of the 50 United States.

Internationally, Dr. Marshall has influenced human and organization performance through his service on the International Board of Standards for Training, Performance, and Instruction (IBSTPI) Board of Directors. Here, his needs assessment-focused research assisted the organization in better understanding its audiences and their needs, as IBSTPI reformulated its long-term strategy and support of learning leaders worldwide. Currently, he is part of an interdisciplinary team retained by the Republic of Georgia's Ministry of Education to advance early childhood education throughout the country.

Learn more at www.jamesmmarshall.com.

The Circle of Strategies

Guerilla Needs Assessment
Creating a Theory of Action
Creating a Logic Model

The Flawed Outcomes Hunt
Developing Successful Outcomes
Setting Priorities: A Dollar for Your Thoughts
Gaining Concensus for Initiaive Outcomes

Finding Your 80/20
Don't Swamp the Boat
Subtracting After You've Added
Phasing Implementation Over Time
Academic Return on Investment

Public Relations Blitz
Strategic Messaging

Triage Tool: Prioritizing Your Crisis Intervention

Failing to "Get Smart" Crisis
Outcome Crisis
Sustainability and Scaling Crisis
Crises
Attention Span Crisis
Things Don't Go as Planned Crisis
Data Crisis

Evaluative Thinking

Making Human Performance Happen
Fidelity Check-up
Backing Your Way Into the Perfect Solution
"Early" Wins
Navigating the White Space

Baking Impact Data Into Your Initiative
Using the Evidence You Already Have
Pursuing Impact Evidence Over Time

When Crisis Strikes

*Our district's bullying prevention program was a great idea. Really, who would disagree with the intent? And yet, two years in, what have we really accomplished? I'm not seeing or hearing anything that suggests we're in a better place bullyingwise. What's worse, I've not heard one mention of the policy from the board or the superintendent's cabinet in months. And now the new survey data are suggesting bullying reports **went up**!*

Sitting in a board meeting and hearing those words from a school board member brings chills to my spine. Those chills would undoubtedly be served with a healthy number of questions that would include the following:

- Were board members part of the original program planning?

- Have they been "brought along" over the past two years, to fully understand the program and its implementation?

- Are there defined outcomes in place? If so, was there agreement about what we would agree is successful program implementation and impact?

- And maybe, even *probably,* reporting going up is a *positive* sign of progress.

- Could the board simply, with a wave of their hands, eliminate a program that, at face value, is desperately needed in today's world?

Bullying, new math, social-emotional learning, professional learning communities, sexual health education, leadership development, ethnic studies. As educators, it is easy to see that initiatives surround us every day. When things go right, we embrace and support them through dedicated and sustained time and energy. Undoubtedly, initiatives require these ingredients and countless others for success—from the implementation angle and from the outcome or impact perspective too.

But all too often, initiatives falter. Maybe things go great early on with the implementation to the point of reaching "cruising altitude." Then, seemingly out of the blue, some force threatens that forward momentum. Other initiatives—including the ones involving great and necessary ideas—never get off the ground. And still others take every hand available to keep things aloft to the point of leaders questioning, is this all worth it?

What's a leader to do when things don't go as planned? Well, my first recommendation is to listen selectively if those around you are panicked, claiming it's a "five alarm fire," or similar. Instead, sit back, take a deep breath, and trust that solutions will come when you're in a space of reflection and intention.

This book is for leaders who seek successful initiatives. Yes—that means it is for all of us! Even more, it is for leaders who want to press the boundaries of success using strategies that are underutilized or not used at all in our schools and districts.

It's also for leaders who want to be "fixers." Many successful leaders are already fixers, whether or not they've accepted that fact. So, this book is also for anyone with a program or initiative facing crisis.

You'll learn to course-correct initiatives in trouble, while also providing insurance for the design and implementation of healthy initiatives that yield predictable results. Here you'll find a mix of evidence-based practices and **ground truth** that offer real solutions to a range of threats faced as initiatives are implemented ... or, as I like to say, when "initiative meets world."

Confessions of an Initiative Leader

I'll be honest: I've had to "fix" most of the initiatives I've led at one time or another. I'll bet you have too. As a program evaluator and thought partner to educational leaders, I plan, implement, and evaluate initiatives all in the spirit of (a) demonstrating their value, and (b) doing everything I can to optimize their return of predictable results for those who participate. Students, teachers, counselors, parents, leaders, regardless of the "who," what matters is that we're able to facilitate positive change for them and for our organizations.

Together, we will explore a range of fates that any initiative may face out in the real world. From lack of results or waning interest and support from leadership, to public relations snafus and other communication-related assaults, you'll review examples—real and hypothetical—and strategies that (a) support your planning of initiatives, and (b) serve as course correction interventions that can be applied when things go, well, not right.

Where to Begin

You may have picked up this book because your initiative has reached a crisis point. That is the initial intent in making it available to leaders. However, it could be you are looking to avoid reaching the crisis point. Some will turn to this book in advance of designing an initiative and use it prophylactically to "bake in" the right conditions under which programs and initiatives thrive. Who you are, and where you stand with an initiative or initiatives that matter to you, will undoubtedly dictate how you proceed.

- If you've reached the point of crisis, spend a bit of time doing triage guided by Planning Your Attack (page 8), and then jump right into the guidance based on the symptoms you and your initiative face.

- If you're looking to understand and avoid some of the often encountered crises I'll cover, then proceeding cover-to-cover is the right path forward.

Regardless of your path, we'll make this snappy! You'll review a finite set of crises that initiatives face along with practical, go-to strategies, born of research and ground truth, that can positively impact the challenges you face, may face, or simply wish to avoid.

Strengthening Your Way Out of Crisis

Admittedly, we're dealing with crisis. When the skies are dark, perhaps the rain is even torrential, it can be hard to find even a patch of blue sky. Even so, let me challenge you to do exactly that as you go about your pursuit of crisis solutions.

Many of us, myself included, have been historically conditioned to first notice what "isn't." Deficit-based gaps are often the default. Of course, deficits exist; they're likely what has driven you to this book—and all is generally right with that trajectory.

But as you move forward in plotting your way out of crisis, take time to note, appreciate, and, most importantly, leverage the strengths you see around you. I've yet to encounter a challenge (or crisis) that didn't exist alongside notable and measurable strengths. In almost every crisis, there are strengths coexisting with the challenge or challenges. Those strengths can be used as strongholds as you work your way out of crisis and into success. Take the time to find these strengths, appreciate them, and use them in your favor, as you seek to combat the headwinds, change their direction, and right the challenges you face. Your path to success is likely to shorten as a result.

Crisis Overview

Before we go too far, it's helpful to quickly lay some groundwork for the crisis-combating work you're about to launch. This first section provides some essential background information about programs and initiatives and a high-level description of the six types of implementation crises we commonly face. Plus, to inform the decision of where to "dive into" this work, there is an assessment you can use to review and prioritize your jumping-off point. Specifically, this Crisis Overview covers the following topics:

- Program or Initiative. What's the Difference?
- When Crisis Strikes: Our Six Types of Crises
- Planning Your Attack: How to Proceed
- Cases and Examples to Inform Your Thinking

Program or Initiative. What's the Difference?

Before we jump into crisis and course corrections, it seems smart to offer a bit of positioning. I've grown fond of the term **initiative** because it best describes the efforts that produce predictable results and measurable impact. *Initiative* is compared to the more traditional term *program,* or *educational program.* Really, programs and initiatives share much in common. At their core, they should be defined efforts that are carefully matched to the intended participants' needs, framed by predefined outcomes, and implemented to bring about predetermined results. So far, so good.

The challenge for education leaders is that we operate within very complex systems. There's no shortage of both programs and initiatives with which we must contend daily. To think that any given program can operate in a vacuum, without attention to the people and systems around it is, well, one great way to reach the point of crisis. So, this is the primary reason for using the term *initiative*. It best reflects reality by describing what it *really* takes to understand, design, implement, and evaluate something that will predictively produce positive change. Whether the initiative involves transitioning educators districtwide to culturally relevant curriculum or trauma-informed care, or engaging students in linked learning pathways or dual immersion or dual enrollment efforts, it's easy to see that success requires a carefully orchestrated effort. For me, that speaks initiative.

Programs Versus Initiatives: There Is a Difference

In *Right From the Start,* I illustrated the difference between program and initiative using the familiar iceberg model (Marshall, 2023). It is included here (Figure 1) to drive home the difference between these two commonly encountered entities.

FIGURE 1 Iceberg Model Comparison of Programs and Initiatives

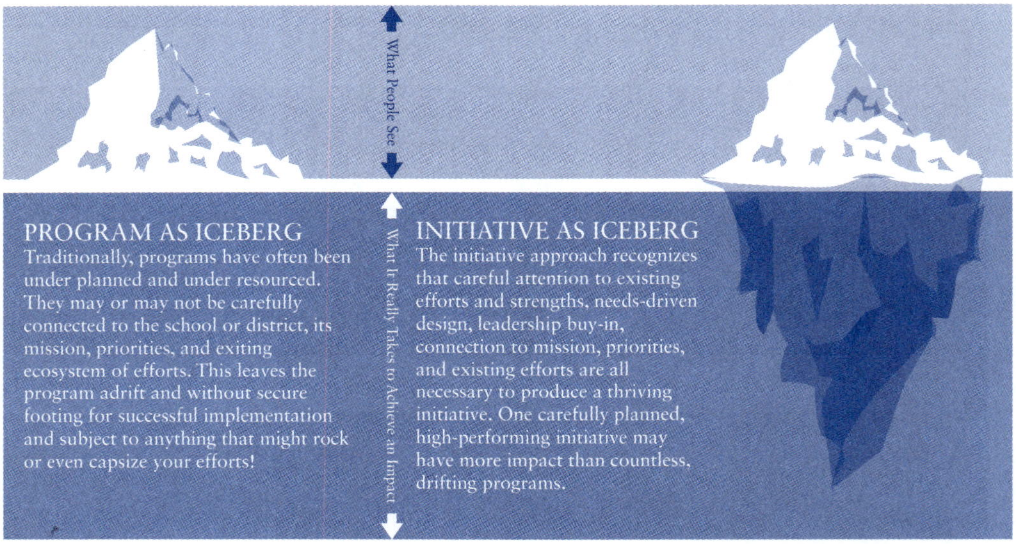

What People See

What It Really Takes to Achieve an Impact

PROGRAM AS ICEBERG
Traditionally, programs have often been under planned and under resourced. They may or may not be carefully connected to the school or district, its mission, priorities, and exiting ecosystem of efforts. This leaves the program adrift and without secure footing for successful implementation and subject to anything that might rock or even capsize your efforts!

INITIATIVE AS ICEBERG
The initiative approach recognizes that careful attention to existing efforts and strengths, needs-driven design, leadership buy-in, connection to mission, priorities, and existing efforts are all necessary to produce a thriving initiative. One carefully planned, high-performing initiative may have more impact than countless, drifting programs.

SOURCE: Marshall (2023).

You'll catch me using the term *program* interchangeably with *initiative* in the pages that follow. And that is perfectly fine if we have a shared understanding of what is required for success, be it a program or an initiative. Your organization's vernacular might not embrace the "initiative" phraseology. If you're facing crisis, now is not the time to begin a terminology reformation campaign! Yet, the eye-popping crises we are about to explore typically stem from programs or initiatives that failed to fully embrace the true range of factors that are requisite for success. Let's move forward with an *initiative* mindset because, by definition, implementing an *initiative* rivets attention to the systemic elements necessary such that predictable outcomes for everyone involved are achieved.

When Crisis Strikes: Six Types of Crises

You've likely picked up this book because you have a program or initiative in crisis. Let's jump into your challenge by defining six types of crises that frame our go-to strategies (Table 1). The chapters that follow go into further detail.

TABLE 1 Crisis Overview—Six Types of Crises

Crisis Type	Short Description
1. Failing to "Get Smart" Crisis	The planning crisis involves no planning, not enough planning, or not the right planning at the start. In the ideal world, the intent is to get smart about the need, people involved, and ideal outcome(s) before determining the initiative's composition.
2. Outcomes Crisis	Defined, overt, measurable, and achievable outcomes provide a guiding "North Star" for any initiative. When outcomes aren't defined, they're vague and lack measurability, they don't describe the impact we truly seek, or they describe an outcome other than the one we want, we face an outcomes crisis.
3. Attention Span Crisis	People get on board early, and then a million other things cross their in-boxes, as requests for support—financial and otherwise—come in. Just six months later, they've already forgotten their commitments to the initiative. This crisis can also occur when attention isn't sustained over time.
4. Data Crisis	Not having the right data, at the right time, for the right purposes. Often, the data piece is like a can kicked down the road, with the design tasks taking priority. Yet, building data into any initiative is something best done as part of the design.
5. When Things Don't Go as Planned Crisis	Implementing programs isn't easy or fast. Even the best-laid, most data-informed initiative designs can still face stormy weather when the "program meets world." When things don't go as planned and implementation stalls, you're facing what I term the D-GAP (don't go as planned) crisis.

(Continued)

TABLE 1 Crisis Overview—Six Types of Crises *(Continued)*

Crisis Type	Short Description
6. Sustaining and Scaling Crisis	Sustaining an initiative long enough to demonstrate its value can be a challenge, as can keeping a successful initiative in place long term. When we find something that works, we want others to benefit. This gives rise to a scaling effort, which typically involves bringing an established program to a wider group of participants. Challenges to either sustaining or scaling an initiative give rise to the sustaining and scaling crisis.

Planning Your Attack: How to Proceed

If a program implementation crisis brought you here, perhaps that crisis is vivid and focused. It may quite plainly be a lack of data to demonstrate the program's value. Yet, when things have gone sideways, more often we face a combination of crises. For example, the attention span crisis is often found alongside many of the other five crises. So, how do you best proceed? Here are three likely scenarios.

1. When one is facing a crisis, your best moves are to understand it, reflect on it, and then develop a responsive solution or set of solutions to improve it. Because you should quickly reach the point of *action,* this book is necessarily snappy. It's designed to swiftly get you there. Thus, you may simply want to read straight through and benefit from an understanding of the full set of crises and the solutions available for their resolution.

2. Now, if the crisis you face is sharply focused, you may want to press forward simply by reviewing the guidance for the crisis you face and working forward to affect improvement using the aligned strategies in the latter half of this book.

3. If you're facing multiple crises, or you're interested in quickly assessing and prioritizing the challenges you face, I suggest you begin by using our first tool, Prioritizing Your Crisis Intervention.

1. Triage Tool: Prioritizing Your Crisis Intervention

The following assessment is designed to help you prioritize your efforts to turn around a faltering program. Here's the scale you'll use to answer each of the following questions. Simply enter a numeric value to reflect your situation in the "Score" column for each statement.

Crisis Level	0	1	2	3	4
Description	Not true for my initiative	A little true for my initiative	A concern for my initiative	An established need to address for my initiative	True crisis—urgent need to address for my initiative

Crisis Assessment Tool

Question	Score	A	B	C	D	E	F
1. We lack a deep understanding of the people for whom this program is targeting.			▓	▓	▓	▓	▓
2. We should have taken more time to define, or benchmark, the current situation.			▓	▓	▓	▓	▓
3. We are unclear about each of the root causes that could explain why there is a problem.			▓	▓	▓	▓	▓
4. We defined what we want our program to achieve, but it's not in measurable terms.		▓		▓	▓	▓	▓
5. When it comes to impact, we've yet to fully elaborate what we want to see from the people involved.		▓		▓	▓	▓	▓
6. We worry that some outcomes may not be achievable or only achievable after many years' time.		▓		▓	▓	▓	▓
7. Our initiative began with interest and support from the higher-ups, but there's been little attention or support of late.		▓	▓		▓	▓	▓
8. We've heard people questioning whether our initiative is worth the investment it requires.		▓	▓		▓	▓	▓
9. We've not successfully promoted our program and its accomplishments; supporters across the school/district are becoming disengaged.		▓	▓		▓	▓	▓
10. We've yet to define the available data or what we should collect, to support of our program's continuous improvement and/or document its accomplishments.		▓	▓	▓		▓	▓
11. Data will come in time, only when the program is more mature.		▓	▓	▓		▓	▓
12. We have people asking us for data to justify our program's existence, but we simply have nothing to offer.		▓	▓	▓		▓	▓
13. We need people to implement the way we designed, in terms of running the program the "right" way.		▓	▓	▓	▓		▓
14. We never anticipated the number of conflicting programs and other things that rivet attention away from the basic work to make this program a success.		▓	▓	▓	▓		▓

Crisis Assessment Tool (continued)

Question	Score	A	B	C	D	E	F
15. While we designed this program to engage, our participants don't seem to care, or they just don't believe they can be successful with it.							
16. We've seen success with this new program, so let's implement it across the district as quickly as possible.							
17. The budget/funding/grant was super helpful getting this initiative off the ground, but we're unsure how we will sustain it in the long run.							
18. There is so much to do, and so little time to do it. We're unsure where to focus our efforts for the greatest program-related impact.							
Totals							

Next, transfer the score value into the available (non-shaded) column for each question. Then, total each lettered column at the base of the worksheet. These columns represent our six types of crises in the following way:

A. Failing to "Get Smart" Crisis
B. Outcomes Crisis
C. Attention Span Crisis
D. Data Crisis
E. When Things Don't Go as Planned Crisis
F. Sustaining and Scaling Crisis

Compare the scores you've established for each of the six columns. At the two extremes:

• A score of zero would suggest there is no evidence of crisis.
• A score of 12, the maximum, indicates what would be a significant crisis.

Contemplate your answers and the compare the values you've achieved and let them guide your next steps. If there are one or two areas that are clear priorities, your best next step may be to read the corresponding chapter(s) for that crisis or crises. If you've evidence of challenges in many areas, consider proceeding forward chapter-by-chapter.

Cases and Examples to Inform Your Thinking

The remainder of this book is dedicated to identifying various initiative crises and then supporting your resolution efforts through tools and checklists. At times you will review examples from my own library of projects and initiatives. We'll also make use of two case studies to illustrate the application of some tools. While the following fictional crises may not match the same challenges you face, they will help you understand the solutions in action. Consider marking this page for quick reference at the points we revisit each of our two cases (Table 2).

TABLE 2   Case Study Profiles

	Example 1: New Elementary Teacher Supports (NETS) Program	Example 2: Fifth-Grade Camp Program
Brief Description	Training and supports for elementary teachers in their first two years of service.	Fifth graders head to a residential camp with their classmates and teachers during their fifth-grade year.
Goal	Reduce the time-to-competency; hasten classroom impact as early as possible.	Experience the outdoors in new ways, grow through outdoor programming while being away from home for a full five days.
Participants	All K–5 educators across the district in their first two years of service.	All fifth-grade students across the district.
Launch	Currently in fourth implementation year.	Program running for 24 years, minus a necessary COVID hiatus.
Current Status Highlights	• Intended as a sort of professional learning community (PLC). • Spotty implementation has plagued the program from its start. • Pockets of success exist, but the successes are not something you can count on reliably or districtwide. • Questions are coming from central office about the program and both its design and cost.	• Costly to implement. • Many parents, administrators, and teachers ask, what really happens at camp? • Some have questioned equity of the experience for teachers, since only 1/13 of the district's teachers participate. • Teachers have asked, "Why must I keep doing this?" and

TABLE 2   Case Study Profiles *(Continued)*

	Example 1: New Elementary Teacher Supports (NETS) Program	Example 2: Fifth-Grade Camp Program
		"Couldn't the paid counselor/teachers at the camp handle it with me?" while suggesting there should be some compensation for working these extra hours while away. • We'll refer to the teachers bringing their fifth-grade students as **teachers,** and the teachers who are permanently assigned and working at the camp as **camp teacher-counselors,** or simply **teacher-counselors.**

The Circle of Strategies

Guerilla Needs Assessment
Creating a Theory of Action
Creating a Logic Model

The Flawed Outcomes Hunt
Developing Successful Outcomes
Setting Priorities: A Dollar for Your Thoughts
Gaining Concensus for Initiaive Outcomes

Triage Tool: Prioritizing Your Crisis Intervention

Failing to "Get Smart" Crisis

Outcome Crisis

Sustainability and Scaling Crisis

Crises

Attention Span Crisis

Things Don't Go as Planned Crisis

Data Crisis

Evaluative Thinking

Finding Your 80/20
Don't Swamp the Boat
Subtracting After You've Added
Phasing Implementation Over Time
Academic Return on Investment

Public Relations Blitz
Strategic Messaging

Making Human Performance Happen
Fidelity Check-up
Backing Your Way Into the Perfect Solution
"Early" Wins
Navigating the White Space

Baking Impact Data Into Your Initiative
Using the Evidence You Already Have
Pursuing Impact Evidence Over Time

Failing to "Get Smart" Crisis

I t's a fact: If you don't know where you're going, anywhere will do. Avoiding that fate means having a plan. As educational leaders, our work is critical. After all, we're leading both educators and the students entrusted to them. Success is the only acceptable outcome. And, for that simple reason, *anywhere* will most certainly *not* do.

Recognizing the Failing to "Get Smart" Crisis

Lack of planning is the most common reason initiatives fail. The planning crisis involves either no planning, not enough planning, or not the right planning on the "front end." By front end, I mean actions we take before the initiative is designed. In the ideal world, this is the time to **get smart**

It's like they don't even know the people who are participating in this program!

Great ideas, but I'm living in a completely different world out here.

What am I supposed to get out of this?

I wish someone had asked me what I need....

I'll participate, but I'm not going to get anything out of it.

None of this matches what my principal is asking us to do.

about the challenge you face, the range of people directly and indirectly involved, and a range of ideal outcomes that, predictably, would improve the situation. We should be getting smart before determining any initiative's composition.

Successful initiatives begin with careful and intentional inquiry into needs. It means "getting smart" about the needs, strengths, people, and setting so that you're making informed decisions that increase the chances you will reap predictable results. What's key is that this happens *before* solutions start getting whipped up.

Solutions to the Failing to "Get Smart" Crisis

Can you retroactively plan for travel once the initiative train has left the station? Even when it is swiftly rolling down the track, perhaps even careening toward a destination you now realize you don't want? Yes, you can! Know that there is no such thing as the perfect program or initiative. If there were, we would have stopped making new ones a long time ago! If you've reached the point of crisis due to planning missteps, it's best to think *evolution* rather than *revolution*. What you don't want to do is simply abandon a potentially impactful initiative before giving it a full chance to demonstrate its value.

Here are the Failing to "Get Smart" tools that will support your way out of this crisis.

- Guerilla Needs Assessment: A "just in time," targeted needs assessment approach to hone your crisis plan of attack

- Creating a Theory of Action: Documenting the relationships between your initiative acts and the outcomes and impacts you expect; basically, the "elevator pitch" for your initiative

- Creating a Logic Model: Detailing the resources your initiative requires, the elements you'll implement, and the outcomes that will result; especially helpful for high-level planning, guidance for initiative design (and course correction), and framing program evaluation

2. Guerilla Needs Assessment

In *Right From the Start* (RFS; Marshall, 2023), I advocate (heavily) for needs assessment. It has so much to contribute to initiatives, and it really helps to ensure success and predictable results. But what if needs assessment didn't happen?

I've described both the symptoms and the challenges, even crises, you may face in this scenario. When there hasn't been needs assessment or there hasn't been enough needs assessment, one solution is to simply get to work and do what should have been done from the start. This strategy is Guerilla Needs Assessment. Table 3 compares the "traditional" and guerilla needs assessment approaches.

TABLE 3 Differences Between Traditional and Guerilla Approaches

RFS (Traditional) Needs Assessment Approach	Guerilla Needs Assessment Approach
1. Someone sees a need (problem, challenge) and defines a "better" state—an ideal, the way things "ought" to be. "Oughts" or "ideals" are helpful *inputs* that can turn into the *outcomes* that frame an initiative. 2. Then, we document how things currently are (actuals, is's), relative to the ideal. 3. The difference between ideal and actual gives us the gap, and the process is termed **gap analysis.** 4. We then explore that gap to understand, in detail, why it exists, including gathering 360-degree perspectives from the people involved. 5. With that clear understanding of causes, we craft a solution, and our initiative design commences.	The differences between the RFS traditional approach I've described, and the *guerilla* approach are ***time*** and ***focus.*** • Do this quick because you're in crisis! • Sharply focus your inquiry on a handful of key things that will help you better understand ideals and current states. And, most important, • Prioritize efforts to understand the situation from participants and their points of view.

Guerilla Needs Assessment differs because of its focus. Setting your focus requires prioritizing the area or areas where you see the greatest challenges. Here are some of the key areas that cause initiatives to go awry alongside helpful guidance for your Guerilla Needs Assessment effort.

	Initiative Crisis Point	How to Proceed
1	Outcomes	• Investigate "ideals" by asking those involved (initiative sponsors, supporters, and participants) to describe the best possible outcome(s). • Challenge those involved to describe the opposite, meaning what *wouldn't* or *would no longer* happen in an ideal outcome. We'll dive into outcomes-related crises soon; for now, note how much outcomes-related issues are contributing to the crisis you face.
2	Participants	Use the 3Vs to connect with participants and understand needs and experiences with the initiative to date. • Voice—Intentionally engage with the diverse voices involved; be an active listener in honor of their sharing their voice. • Viewpoint—Pursue understanding of participants' lived experiences and how they intersect with the initiative; set aside your preconceptions and assumptions and embrace the views of your participants. • Vision—Invite participants to co-create (or co-correct) the initiative by asking for their ideas about the ideal (implementation, outcome) moving forward.
3	Barriers to Initiative Alignment	• Based on the barrier(s) your participants face, consider the alignment between those barrier(s) and the elements your initiative involves. • Confirm that, for each barrier type faced, the initiative includes a matched component designed to positively affect and improve that barrier. See the Making Human Performance Happen tool (page 84) for a summary of the human performance barrier types and for questions that uncover barriers at play.
4	Outcomes-to-Implementation Alignment	• Compare the outcomes you've defined to the implementation currently being implemented. • Determine where there is, and isn't, direct alignment between the initiative's components and the outcomes it requires. • Use the logic model building tool to detail your initiative's logic, and confirm the alignment among resources, initiative elements you're implementing, and the outcomes you target.

Here's a grid to document what you currently know about actuals, ideals, causes, and strengths. Then, describe the most important information that is currently missing and that will be the focus of your Guerilla Needs Assessment effort.

Needs Assessment Information	Your Current Understanding	Priority Information to Be Obtained Quickly (via Guerilla Needs Assessment)
Actuals		
Ideals		
Causes		
Strengths		

The New Elementary Educator Supports (NETS) leadership team conducted a preliminary meeting to take stock of their current crisis and to plan next steps. Some sample Guerilla Needs Assessment planning results from the NETS team are shared here.

Needs Assessment Information	Your Current Understanding	Priority Information to Be Obtained Quickly (via Guerilla Needs Assessment)
Actuals	• Surveys from participating teachers give the program mixed reviews in terms of helping them be a "success with teaching their students." • Roughly half of the eligible teachers make use of NETS in any given year. • When asked, elementary school principals vary in their awareness and understanding of NETS, including about 33% who are unaware the program exists.	• Review channels by which NETS is promoted at both the site leader and new teacher levels. • Collect rapid feedback through quick and targeted (>10 questions) survey with eligible teachers and elementary site leaders to determine awareness, reasons for/against participation, and beliefs about NETS program value. • Collect rapid feedback through quick and targeted (>10 questions) survey with NETS program completers to uncover program strengths, limitations, and opportunities not yet realized.
Ideals	• Teachers build community with others in their first two years of teaching. • NETS participants receive support in areas of need to thrive in the classroom. • NETS contributes to retention during a new teacher's first years, when they are most likely to leave the profession.	• Define, in tangible, measurable terms, what we'll take as evidence of achieving "success with teaching their students" so there is a common understanding and progress can be measured. • Similarly, define "build community" to establish shared expectations and review program/implementation design for alignment with that definition. • Determine progress toward retention by pulling teacher data from past seven years, and identify any differences before, and following, NETS (differentiate by participation level, where possible).

Needs Assessment Information	Your Current Understanding	Priority Information to Be Obtained Quickly (via Guerilla Needs Assessment)
Causes	• Program was originally designed because of high elementary school teacher attrition in Years 2 through 5. • Program was predicated on the belief that teachers leave because they lack support and connection to other new teaching professionals.	• Review the "why" to confirm original assumptions. Each program leadership team member will conduct a brief interview with five new teachers to understand their experiences more deeply. • Attempt to quantify the amount of need for pedagogical support versus the need for community and connection. Which should take precedence?
Strengths	• A commitment to increase retention in the district and the profession. • Recognition that the program isn't having the impact it should and a desire to pursue data-driven modifications	• Inquiry, as outlined above, is designed to also identify program strengths. • Acknowledge that further definition of program outcomes (impact) is needed, with consensus, such that the full team (program leaders, site leaders, new teachers) have a shared understanding of the program and what they can realistically expect from participation.

3. Creating a Theory of Action

Leaders with an initiative in crisis due to a lack of planning may need to "zoom out" and get a fresh perspective on exactly what they set out to do. The Theory of Action is one of two tools that can be used to document the thinking, intentions, and outcomes that guide an initiative's design by doing the following:

- Summarizing the range of things the initiative will require to be done alongside what we can expect to see happen as a result of accomplishing those tasks

- Supporting initiative planning as you iteratively define and refining your actions in support of the desired outcome or outcomes

- Elaborating how you plan to get from where you are today, to the better state of being you've described, through your planned initiative

There's a difference between that and a logic model. A **theory of action** is necessarily high level, while a logic model (our next strategy) is usually more detailed. The theory of action elaborates *why* something will happen, while the logic model details *what* will be done. The theory of action works as an early intervention to define your team's thinking and press toward consensus around the *how, what,* and *why* of your initiative in crisis.

Use the Theory of Action tool:

- In a crisis stage. When early planning hasn't been accomplished and perspectives regarding the initiative's design and operation are neither clear nor shared, it may be necessary to take a significant step back and collaboratively create a theory of action.

- As a grounding opportunity. Challenging the team to describe the initiative, how it is supposed to work, what it is intended to do, and the longer-term impact it is designed to have can be insightful.

- To explore and understand—current levels of clarity and consensus (or lack thereof), along with levels of support across your various program partners, implementers, collaborators.

Use this template to draft a Theory of Action for your initiative by following the prompts as indicated. Note that a Theory of Action can have more than three steps. Review the examples here and elsewhere to discover flexibility in ways this helpful tool can be produced.

1	If we take these actions . . .

Your Initiative's Planned Work:
The actions you will perform, the things you will implement, that comprise your planned initiative

-
-
-
-
-
-

2	Then we can expect this to happen . . .

Your Initiative's Outcomes:
The things you expect your initiative participants to realize through their participation

-
-
-
-
-
-

3	And, as a result, this will lead to . . .

Your Initiative's Ultimate Impact:
The ultimate impact of this work, from your school or district's perspective

-
-
-
-
-

This example Theory of Action uses the NETS program case study and depicts the program upon reaching the point of crisis.

1	If we . . .

Your Initiative's Planned Work:
The actions you will perform, the things you will implement, that comprise your planned initiative

- Engage with, and establish professional learning communities for first- and second-year elementary teachers.
- Bring them together three times a year.
- Provide pedagogical training and supports.

2	Then we can expect . . .

Your Initiative's Outcomes:
The things you expect your initiative participants to realize through their participation

- Connections are made between and among early career teachers, both within their schools and across the district.
- Teachers improve their efficacy in providing instruction to our youngest students.
- Deep, informal support networks between and among teachers are established and conversations regularly occur.

3	And as a result, this will lead to . . .

Your Initiative's Ultimate Impact:
The ultimate impact of this work, from your school or district's perspective

Teachers who
- possess a deep love of teaching,
- choose to remain in the field and their classroom position at least five years,
- exhibit a high level of confidence in their instructional duties, and
- demonstrate the impact of their love of teaching, confidence, and pedagogical prowess as reflected in their students' academic and social-emotional performance, as well as the overall classroom culture.

Crisis-related elements to note:

- While the outcomes and impact statements are on the right track, the planned work lacks sufficient detail to fully explain the program and set expectations around implementation, including being able to determine if it is happening with fidelity to the plan.
- Additional detail to make both outcomes and impacts measurable (overt, observable such that two people could agree they have, or haven't been realized) would strengthen this theory of action.

Here's a second example Theory of Action using the Fifth-Grade Camp program case study, developed at the point of crisis.

1	If we . . .

Your Initiative's Planned Work:
The actions you will perform, the things you will implement, that comprise your planned initiative

- Require all fifth-grade students to attend a week-long, in-residence camp.
- Offer a camp program that combines elements of STEM, physical education, team building, and outdoor enrichment.

2	Then we can expect . . .

Your Initiative's Outcomes:
The things you expect your initiative participants to realize through their participation

- Students will discover a new independence, being away from home for a full week.
- Camp will ignite a passion for the outdoors, especially for students from key urban schools who are unfamiliar with rural environments.
- Students will make new connections, as they apply STEM and physical education content in new and novel settings.

3	And as a result, this will lead to . . .

Your Initiative's Ultimate Impact:
The ultimate impact of this work, from your school or district's perspective

- A love of the outdoors
- Memories of a positive outdoor, nontraditional learning experience
- A lived experience they would not otherwise have, which they can carry throughout their lifetime and use to connect with others

Crisis-related elements to note:

- Planned work elements are especially high-level and need further elaboration to fully understand what will happen, such that all agree on the implementation.
- Outcomes are unhelpfully vague and, as such, lack measurability. For example, how would you measure a "discovered new independence" or "an ignited passion"?
- Impact statements are aspirational, but it is largely impossible to understand or have confidence as to how they will come about from the work and outcomes sections. Again, making things overt and measurable is key.

4. Creating a Logic Model

Background: If your initiative has reached the crisis point as a result of a lack of planning, or because the people involved are simply not aligned with the program design, implementation, or outcomes, building a **logic model** can support any effort to calibrate.

Successful initiatives are intentional. They respond to needs, set targets through outcomes, and then proceed with an implementation that is responsive to needs and outcomes alike. When this logic is strong and we reach the point of measuring impact, we know what we're looking for: Essentially, it is a confirmation of achieving the outcomes we defined, which points back to the fact that needs were addressed and satisfied.

What I've just described is the "logic" behind an initiative, and a logic model is one of the best tools leaders can use to support initiative design and implementation. Logic models present a concentrated picture of a program or initiative by depicting:

- the resources the initiative requires,

- the processes the initiative's implementation involves and metrics by which we'll confirm the implementation's successful momentum (termed *outputs*), and

- the outcomes the initiative is designed to bring about for participants as a result of its success (often defined and organized in short-, medium-, and long-term outcome categories).

A logic model can help you realize the following things:

- Clarity—by elaborating the necessary resource investments, initiative components and implementation measures, and targeted outcomes

- Collaboration—by helping leaders and contributors document and evolve current thinking in a condensed, typically one-page, summary of the initiative's current design

- Consensus—by using the logic model to socialize the initiative's design and intended impact for purposes of gaining agreement across your team and those who must support the initiative

As you move forward out of crisis, use the logic model as both roadmap and placemat:

- Use it as a roadmap to guide the initiative's (re)design and implementation, while also defining the initiative's impact, which focuses our watch for outcomes.

- Use it as a placemat whenever you're meeting to discuss the initiative. Put the current logic model in front of each collaborator so that your team is literally "on the same page" as the discussion begins.

If your initiative isn't yet represented in some form of a logic model, this template will help make that happen.

Logic Model Template				
Inputs	**Implementation**		**Outcomes**	
	Processes	**Outputs**	**Short-Term**	**Long-Term/Impact**
Your Planned Work			Your Intended Results	
Guidance: Inputs describe the resources that will be directed toward the initiative. You might also think about inputs as the "investments" made in the initiative. Consider human, financial, and organizational resources.	Processes are the things that will be accomplished to implement the initiative. Processes describe how the initiative will use the inputs (resources). Consider the intentional program activities, including tools, training, and events, that, together, are designed to bring about the outcomes.	Processes lead to outputs. Outputs are metrics by which we can assess the initiative's implementation progress, including implementation fidelity.	Short-term outcomes, sometimes referenced as "outputs," typically describe accomplishment of the defined processes. Consider what might provide the earliest evidence that the program is having even the most limited impact. Short-term outcomes are typically those things that point to "promising results," which lead to longer-term impact.	Long-term outcomes stem from the goals of the initiative and the needs the initiative was intended to address. These outcomes should describe positive change for the people your initiative will reach. Consider growth in knowledge or skills, positive changes in attitudes or confidence levels (self-efficacy), and desired changes for your participants' actions (performance).

Here is the draft logic model example, as might be developed by the NETS initiative team.

Logic Model Draft: NETS, Page 1				
Inputs	**Implementation**		**Outcomes**	
	Processes	**Outputs**	**Short-Term**	**Long-Term/Impact**
	Your Planned Work		Your Intended Results	
• Data that reveal a more than 50% attrition rate for elementary teachers new to the profession • Research around effective practice supporting new elementary-level teachers • Leadership commitment to the NETS initiative resources—personnel and budget	• Training: Three times a year professional development targeted to (1) pedagogy, (2) classroom management. and (3) collective efficacy • Professional learning communities (PLCs): Site-based PLCs overseen by site leaders and specifically positioned to engage, excite, and encourage teachers new to the school • Resources: New teacher just-in-time supports around teaching and classroom management, frequent tips in a biweekly newsletter to new teacher-participants	• Three trainings held per year, one in each identified topical area • All NETS teachers attend each training • PLCs operate at each school • New teachers attend and find the experience valuable Resources are distributed to teachers; teachers make repeated use of resources; newsletter is delivered twice a month; teachers find value in its content	• New teachers can describe, and their classroom practice demonstrates, new approaches to teaching (pedagogy), classroom management, and collective efficacy • New teachers can describe their reasons for entering the profession and can point to tangible accomplishments in their classroom • New teachers incrementally raise their confidence in diverse areas of practice, including pedagogy, management, parent involvement, PLC efforts, etc.	• New teachers remain in the field, at the elementary school level, for at least five years • Results of culture and climate surveys, as well as socioemotional and academic indicators, reflect high levels of success in their work with students • Teachers sustain, or deepen, their love of the profession, as measured by their persistence, descriptions of why they teach, and completion of ongoing personal and professional development

This draft logic model example presents the initiative as might be developed by the Fifth-Grade Camp team.

Logic Model Draft: Fifth-Grade Camp, Page 1				
Inputs	**Implementation**		**Outcomes**	
	Processes	**Outputs**	**Short-Term**	**Long-Term/Impact**
Your Planned Work			Your Intended Results	
• Research on benefits of environmental education and wellness, specific to the outdoors and conservation, plus active and authentic learning • Fewer than 35% of inner-city youth, especially those from low-income households, experience nature in deep ways • District leadership commitment to the camp program, including human resources, infrastructure, and necessary budget allocation	• Logistics: Fifth-grade teachers plan, fundraise as necessary, and ensure their students' readiness and full participation in camp • Camp: All fifth-grade students in the district will attend a one-week, in-residence camp program with their teacher and class • Curriculum: Camp counselor-teachers implement a camp-based learning experience for fifth graders that involves content areas of STEM, physical education, and team building	• Teachers complete all planning tasks • Each fifth-grade student and their teacher attends a five-day camp at some point in the academic year • Camp counselor-teachers implement the curriculum as planned	• Students show up ready to fully engage in camp • Students enjoy their camp experience • Student confidence in being away from home, along with their personal direction for day-to-day self-supportive tasks, increases by the end of the camp experience • Students demonstrate a passion for the outdoors • Students make new connections between curriculum content and its real-world application in the outdoors in ways that are not possible in the classroom • Students take pride in their camp service contributions and helping others	• A sustained love of the outdoors • A new appreciation for the real-world application of key discipline content, such as science and math • A lived experience students continue to talk about for years to come • Fifth-grade students will choose to participate in a local conservation task within one year of attending camp

	Implementation		Outcomes	
Inputs	**Processes**	**Outputs**	**Short-Term**	**Long-Term/Impact**
	Your Planned Work		Your Intended Results	
	• Program: Students engage in camp activities and lessons, plus enjoy self-selected free time activities, during their five days at camp	• Students choose to engage fully and complete camp activities • Students choose positive free-time activities related to the camp setting that sustain and extend their learning in targeted areas		
	• Service: Students help operate the camp by leading activities for their classmates, engaging in meal prep and clean-up, and participating in environmental stewardship activities	• Students choose to support the camp through their active participation in camp-required service tasks		

Logic Model Draft: Fifth-Grade Camp, Page 2

Compared to NETS, this logic model is far less developed and effective at this draft stage. Just some of the signs you may have noted that may point to potential crisis ahead are as follows:

• Note the lack of detail specific to processes, which then causes vague outputs.

• That detail is especially lean for the camp curriculum, upon which much of the outcomes must rely if they're to be realized.

• Without specific processes and outputs, the program's design and implementation expectations are unclear. This challenges fidelity of program implementation.

• Outcomes are often vague, which means two people might interpret them differently, and many are not measurable as stated.

• While true for both short- and long-term outcomes, the long-term outcomes are especially vague, meaning we have no way of confirming the program is meeting expectations, let alone justifying the investment.

• Additionally, since the team is experiencing challenges specific to the role (and required presence) of the classroom teacher, it would likely be important to further define that role and consider defining outcomes for their participation, just like their students.

Outcomes Crisis

Outcomes, for educators, are our coin of the realm! And, without them, we are penniless. OK—hear me out.

If we were Elon Musk, our coin of the realm would be, well, coins—as in cryptocurrency or plain old dollars in the bank. Perhaps, were I a tad more magnanimous, I could say "building shareholder value" is the coin of the realm in that setting. And we would measure success, initially, by the number of cars sold, tunnels bored, or more simply landing on the moon. But, ultimately, the bank account balance reflects the coin of the realm.

But an educator's work is multidimensional. Empowering teachers and developing the minds and abilities of all students are core to that work. But below that global level, and especially when pursuing a given initiative, it is through outcomes that we define purpose, elaborate success criteria, and rally our investment toward shared and agreed outcomes.

What, exactly, are we trying to accomplish here?

I thought we were targeting growth in reading, but teachers are saying it's social emotional-learning they're pressing.

I thought everyone would have to demonstrate their skills before we considered them.

Do we even know what "appreciate the applications of STEM in the community" means?

Where are the success criteria that tells us what we're looking for?

Students are asking, "Why are we even studying this?"

Recognizing the Outcomes Crisis

Can you imagine a situation in which an initiative is launched with no defined outcomes? It happens far more often than you might think. I see it more frequently with teacher professional development initiatives, and less often with student-focused initiatives. Perhaps that's because we're so accustomed to defining learning outcomes for students. Yet, when our attention turns to adults, that best practice is often set aside.

When outcomes haven't been defined, you are then left, literally, with a program where any sort of result *might* equal success. That's not the business we educators are in. This lack of definition hastens crisis. For example, try measuring the impact of your initiative when you have no idea what you're looking for!

Strategies to Address the Outcomes Crisis

Don't be discouraged if you're facing the outcomes challenge; this crisis is truly an opportunity.[1] This may be the time to revisit the outcomes you currently have and apply some course correction strategy. People do this all the time. If you've not defined measurable outcomes, that should become your priority.

Addressing an Outcomes Crisis involves getting good at spotting and understanding the flaws from which outcomes typically suffer. That identification task is naturally followed by revising those that are troublesome, followed by an effort that gains consensus on the revised set of outcomes.

Regardless of whether you're creating or revising outcomes, make sure to circle back and gather consensus for your newly minted outcomes from all parties with interest in your initiative.

Here are the Outcomes Crisis tools that will support your way out of this crisis.

- The Flawed Outcomes Hunt: Common issues with outcomes to inform review of existing outcomes and avoid pitfalls for outcomes you develop

- Developing Successful Outcomes: Key components of successful outcomes to guide their creation for your own initiative

- Setting Priorities: A Dollar for Your Thoughts: Creative, collaborative approach to use for prioritizing your initiative's focus and, especially, its outcomes

- Gaining Consensus for Initiative Outcomes: Approaches for sharing your initiative's plan for purposes of establishing buy-in with necessary supporters and constituencies

---

[1]Spoiler alert: Every crisis is an opportunity! They're opportunities to continuously improve your initiatives. Plus, when viewed appreciatively (through **appreciative inquiry**), they're amazing opportunities to improve **yourself as a leader,** as you learn from the situation and apply your understanding and judgment to the benefit of everyone involved.

5. The Flawed Outcomes Hunt

What if you have outcomes, but they're just not the right ones? Flawed outcomes often result when needs assessment hasn't happened, or it hasn't gone deep enough to fully understand the situation. As a result, you haven't produced meaningful outcomes or developed consensus across the full range of people involved in the initiative, from the implementers to leaders whose support is necessary for the initiative's ongoing existence. Another scenario leading to this type of crisis is simply your evolution of thought as you lead the initiative, which can result in outdated outcomes that no longer match needs.

How will you recognize flawed outcomes when you see them? Here are some examples to color your thinking and inform your hunt. Use this checklist to review your outcomes against eight commonly encountered outcomes flaws.

Use this checklist to review your outcomes and spot those that need improvement. You'll also find it useful for quality control once you've defined outcomes and want to make certain they're effective.

	Flaw	You'll Know It by . . .
1	Goal acting as Outcome	Goals are broad statements of intent and, typically, our initiatives are framed by goals. However, if your outcomes are written as goals, they are likely flawed. More on that below.
2	Scope— Incomplete	Outcomes fail to describe the full range of impacts the initiative has been created to bring about.
3	Scope— Overreach	Outcomes go beyond what's reasonable to expect, based upon the initiative currently being implemented.
4	People	Outcomes are written for the wrong people, or outcomes have not been developed for the full range of individuals involved. For example, outcomes for students participating in the initiative are present, but outcomes for teachers in terms of their implementation of the new initiative haven't been defined.
5	Focus	Outcomes describe impacts that, in hindsight, are not the true—or priority— focus of the implemented initiative.
6	Level	Outcomes are written at a superficial level rather than the true "terminal" impact you wish to have for initiative participants. Outcomes might describe the means rather than the ends. For example, outcomes describe the different activities in which participants will engage rather than the results that will come from successful participation.
7	Feasibility	Currently defined outcomes are impossible to achieve through the initiative being implemented. For example, outcomes describe impacts that go beyond what is reasonable to expect from the initiative's implementation.
8	Measurability	Outcomes, as currently stated, are impossible to measure. For example, there is no way to demonstrate achievement of the outcomes as stated. Therefore, the initiative's impact cannot be proven.

It's critical to distinguish *goals* from *outcomes*. *Goals* are broad statements of intent. Some examples would be reducing bullying, improving students' reading ability, developing an appreciation for democracy, or increasing family connections and involvement. Each of these goals isn't measurable as stated; each could mean many things. They could be interpreted in different ways, by different people. Goals are helpful in giving a sense of general direction. Yet alone, they are insufficient. *Outcomes* provide the next level of detail that lets us collaboratively picture and agree upon exactly what will signal achievement of our stated goal or goals.

6. Developing Successful Outcomes

If you've already reviewed your outcomes and discovered some that are flawed, it's time to pursue fixes. You likely noted the key elements that make for successful outcomes as part of your hunt for those outcomes that aren't yet ready to fully perform.

Having well-written, specific outcomes offers many benefits that include.

- providing a clear, public **declaration of purpose,** specific to results the initiative will return;

- serving as the means to **gain consensus around success** and how we'll know it when we see it;

- guiding for kinds of **strategies** the initiative will employ;

- informing the **validation/evaluation,** and

- helping **scaffold participant attention and the press for learning** by communicating expectations for participation.

I recommend using the often-referenced SMART criteria to guide outcome authoring and improvement. First defined by Doran (1981), these elements are commonly applied to learning outcomes and success criteria to achieve the benefits.

Below are two examples of successful outcomes. Compare them to the criteria below.
- New elementary school teachers will remain in the profession for a minimum of five years.
- Fifth-grade students will choose to participate in a local conservation task within one year of attending camp.

	Criteria	Description	Examples
1	Specific	State in specific terms what will happen and the people who will achieve the outcome.	Specific: • People: New elementary teachers, fifth-grade students • What will happen: Stay in the profession, participate in a local conservation task
2	Measurable	Describes an outcome that is measurable rather than a broad or abstract construct that is difficult or impossible to measure.	• Measurable: Continued employment in the elementary teaching field, participation in a local conservation task • Not measurable examples: Continuing to love teaching, being motivated to teach, expressing a love of the environment, new appreciation for the outdoors
3	Attainable	Effective outcomes describe something that is possible to achieve, using the resources available.	• Attainable: Continued employment, participation in conservation task • Not attainable: Stopping all elementary teachers from leaving the field, changing their peers' perspectives of the environment
4	Relevant	Is closely aligned with the initiative's overall intent and relevant to the intended participants.	• Relevant: Continued employment aligns perfectly with initiative goal, participation in conservation task would demonstrate impact of fifth-grade camp learning (cognitive and affective)
5	Time Certain	Has a time frame and is possible to achieve within that defined time frame.	• Time certain: Continued employment for **five years**, participation in conservation task **within one year** • Not achievable: Remain an elementary teacher for life; participate in conservation efforts through high school

A final note about outcomes: Outcomes are essentially the "connective tissue" between needs and the initiative's design. When successfully defined, outcomes respond to the needs of the people involved while also directing the very strategies our initiative will employ to bring those outcomes about. Suffice it to say, when outcomes are ill- or poorly-defined, your initiative's destination is far from certain.

7. Setting Priorities: A Dollar for Your Thoughts

If your outcomes crisis is being caused by having too many outcomes or a lack of focus across the outcomes you've defined, consider the Dollar for Your Thoughts strategy. Part priority setting, part consensus building, this process involves getting everyone in the same room and pressing for clarity and consensus, as well as priorities, around the outcomes your initiative will commit to bringing about.

The following tool will guide you through this exercise.

Use this tool when you face too many outcomes and need to prioritize the possibilities. When implemented correctly, you'll also gain estimates of consensus for the group that does the rating.

	Step	What You'll Do
1	Gather a strategic group of initiative shareholders.	Get creative about who you want around the table. Think about those with deep knowledge of the challenge you're addressing, those who will implement the program, and those who must support it through the dedication of resources.
2	Surface a range of outcomes the initiative could/should address.	You may already have a list of outcomes that are currently guiding your initiative in crisis. If so, list and number them for distribution to your group.

If you have not defined outcomes, you'll want to begin by creating a blue-sky list of possible outcomes that your initiative could pursue. |
| 3 | "Fund" your participants. | Tell each participant that they have $100 and ask them to make their investments in the outcomes. |
| 4 | Assign value to each outcome on the numbered list. | Participants distribute their $100 across the list of outcomes. |
| 5 | Tally the investment results. | Take all submitted values and establish an average and standard deviation for each question.

The average provides an indication of the relative value of each question to the group of collaborators. The standard deviation helps illustrate the level of consensus in your group. |
| 6 | Share the results and review as a group. | Share the resulting average and standard deviation for each outcome and challenge your group to make observations:
• Where is there consensus?
• Where is there lack of agreement?
• Are there surprises?
• Where do priorities seem to lie?
• Was something significant overlooked that needs to be added? |
| 7 | Work to consensus about outcomes. | As discussion ebbs and flows, press for consensus among the group about the following:
• What objectives should be pursued
• Any outcomes that can be set aside
• Additional outcomes that should be added but are yet to be defined |
| 8 | Confirm the final list. | Ask the group, "If each of these outcomes was realized by our participants, would we agree that needs had been met and the challenge to which our initiative responds has been fully addressed?"

If not, return to Step 7 and revise your list until a final list is confirmed. |

Here is a worksheet you can use to record results of your exercise. The Average Contribution will be the average of all team members' assigned values. Adding the Standard Deviation will help you see how much consensus is represented in that average contribution. You can easily copy the table into Excel to quickly determine both average and standard deviation. Remember, a relatively high standard deviation suggests less consensus; a low standard deviation suggests the opposite.

Outcome	Record Each Team Member's Dollar Contributions					Average Contribution	Standard Deviation (Consensus)
List outcomes below	1	2	3	4	5	Calculate	Calculate
1.							
2.							
3.							
4.							
5.							
6.							
7.							
8.							
9.							
10.							

Using our NETS case study, here is an abbreviated example of what might result from the Dollar for Your Thoughts exercise. As you can see, some clear priorities were established. The results can then be used to discuss and come to agreement about focus.

Outcome (Short-Term Outcomes: Original List for Team Member Rating)	Record Each Team Member's Dollar Contributions					Average	Standard Deviation (Consensus)
	1	2	3	4	5	Calculate	Calculate
1. New teachers can describe their reasons for entering the profession and can point to tangible accomplishments in their classroom.	$30.00	$25.00	$19.00	$25.00	$15.00	$22.80	$5.85
2. New teachers can describe, and their classroom practice demonstrates, new approaches to teaching (pedagogy), classroom management, and collective efficacy.	$15.00	$25.00	$20.00	$25.00	$15.00	$20.00	$5.00
3. New teachers incrementally raise their confidence in diverse areas of practice, including pedagogy, management, parent involvement, PLC efforts, etc.	$15.00	$20.00	$15.00	$25.00	$14.00	$17.80	$4.66
4. New teachers incrementally increase their love of teaching (expressed qualitatively in interviews), as their expertise and experience grow.	$10.00	$10.00	$15.00	$25.00	$4.00	$12.80	$7.85
5. Given a typical classroom/student challenge, new teachers can describe an effective strategy to address.	$10.00	$20.00	$15.00	$0.00	$4.00	$9.80	$8.07
6. New teachers are a leading voice in their site's PLCs.	$10.00	$0.00	$0.00	$0.00	$20.00	$6.00	$8.94
7. Each new teacher inspires another teacher to remain in the profession.	$0.00	$0.00	$10.00	$0.00	$20.00	$6.00	$8.94
8. New teachers give high ratings to each of the professional development sessions.	$5.00	$0.00	$3.00	$0.00	$4.00	$2.40	$2.30
9. New teachers talk to at least three new people at each convening.	$0.00	$0.00	$3.00	$0.00	$4.00	$1.40	$1.95

Outcome (Short-Term Outcomes: Original List for Team Member Rating)	Record Each Team Member's Dollar Contributions					Average	Standard Deviation (Consensus)
	1	2	3	4	5	Calculate	Calculate
10. New teachers can describe the PLC process.	$5.00	$0.00	$0.00	$0.00	$0.00	$1.00	$2.24

- This is a list of the 10 original, short-term outcomes. The team made their investments and totaled things up.
- A natural "break point" was observed, causing the first five outcomes to be adopted, which are shown in our earlier NETS Logic Model example.
- The remaining outcomes were set aside, as lesser priority. In time, the team could return and reconsider once they have data to inform the initiative's evolution and continuous improvement efforts.

8. Gaining Consensus for Initiative Outcomes

Gaining consensus on our initiative's outcomes is equal parts strategy and necessity. You gotta do it. Hard stop. When consensus isn't reached early on in the planning stages, you're asking for trouble. From disagreements about outcomes—what's priority, what matters, what's "right"—to lack of, or waning, support when you fail to gain consensus about the initiative early on, you've set yourself up for crisis down the road.

Your Guerilla Needs Assessment may lead to revised outcomes. A basic review of flawed outcomes may also lead to revision. And any of these changes may also trigger modifications to the initiative focus or its implementation.

Whatever the course correction, you must include an intentional effort to gain consensus of the initiative team and supporters—those responsible for leading and implementing, and the people whose support the initiative requires (the superintendent, other senior leaders, the board of education). Use this opportunity to get everyone on the same page and agreeing in the following areas.

The task is a basic setting of expectations, with a healthy dose of calibrating expectations, all done with intention.

If this didn't happen with your initiative early on, don't make the same mistake at the point of crisis. If it did happen early on, but you're now working to course-correct due to any form of crisis, consider (re)gaining consensus a necessary step at this point.

The following checklist frames six dimensions of consensus and offers descriptions of each. Work with your team to explore, discuss, negotiate, and then agree on each dimension specific to your initiative work.

	Area	Reach consensus on
1	Focus	The initiative's focus and intended participants
2	Outcomes	Outcomes the initiative will pursue for participants and agreement about the evidence required to prove their attainment
3	Implementation	How the initiative will be implemented and metrics to gauge progress along the way
4	Impact	The initiative's intended impact across the organization
5	Evidence	The full set of evidence you will collect and monitor to demonstrate impact over time
6	Timeline to Results	Setting expectations about what results will be reported, and when each reporting will happen, making sure to accommodate both implementation-related and outcomes-related results

Each of the above areas will require some predetermination of your initiative plan, along with pre-collection of documents and other supporting resources that you will share with the group, use to illustrate the initiative, and bring people to the "same page," literally. Here's a list of likely tools and resources, most of which are addressed in this book, that you'll want to use as inputs to your consensus-development effort.

- Theory of Action: overarching picture of the initiative that succinctly plots what you'll do to get from where you are today to the better state you've defined, as a result of your initiative's implementation.
- Logic Model: helpfully defines implementation components, expected outputs, and outcomes
- List of Outcomes: short-, mid-, and long-term outcomes for all participants of your initiative
- Standards or Benchmarks: from district, state, or national levels, and including professional organization recommendations
- Project Plan: Essentially, the "bible" for the program containing many of the above-referenced components, along with detailed implementation plans, budget, resource allocations, and an evaluation plan (see my book *Right From the Start* for guidance in building one for your initiative [Marshall, 2023]).

Attention Span Crisis

Your initiative's design was flawless. Based on thorough needs assessment, you and your team carefully crafted an initiative and proceeded with implementation. In fact, all seemed to be going just fine six months in. Then, unsuspectedly one day, you receive an email questioning the ongoing investment in personnel and facilities. You're asked for evidence that there was a measurable return to justify the ongoing investment. Shocked, you immediately questioned how this could be happening: It's only been six months!

Why did we even commit to this program in the first place?

We've been waiting six months and there are still no impact data.

Are we even on the right track?

Aren't we already investing in [insert name of program]? Do we really need this?

There's gotta be other programs that could accomplish this faster.

Recognizing the Attention Span Crisis

The Attention Span Crisis is common and easy to understand. People get on board early, they back the plan you've worked hard to create, and then they forget it, leaving you to go off into the world and do good work. A million other things then cross their in-boxes, as requests for support—financial and otherwise—come in.

Yet, when you've been working the initiative day-to-day, it's hard to believe they've already forgotten their commitments. And seriously, return-on-investment results in just six months?

It's not unusual, or unreasonable, for leaders above you to need justification for initiative investments. The crisis comes when their expectations haven't been addressed and managed from the start. If that doesn't happen, the initiative becomes an easy target for challenges. When it comes to setting and managing expectations with initiatives, this is *not* the time to "set it and forget it!" Rather, set it and then follow through on the assumption that buy-in and support must be earned and regularly re-earned. Table 4 describes the oft-encountered attention span crises.

TABLE 4 Types of Attention Span Crises

Buy-in	Results Need Time to Bake
Buy-in is often a covert challenge. You might not even know it is happening until it is almost too late. Your initiative relies on the support of many people, which include those at the top level of your organization who must support it, the people responsible for its implementation, and those who are your active participants. Buy-in-related challenges happen when (a) you haven't taken the time to gain the support of all three groups, and/or (b) your initially established buy-in isn't sustained, to the point that people begin questioning the initiative's very existence. Again, you've lost the positive attention that fuels successful initiatives.	How many times have I heard, "But the state test is only given once a year!" Of course, there are countless ways to justify an initiative's worth at every stage of implementation. Yet for those unfamiliar with your initiative, *results—or lack of results*—may be the cause of an Attention Span Crisis. You'll know this when you receive requests to justify costs with evidence of impact. "What are you doing with this program to justify three full-time staff?" "How do we know, even if we keep funding this work, it's going to make a difference?" If you're frustrated by this kind of Attention Span Crisis, you're in good company. As educators, we know it takes time, often more time than people are initially ready to commit, to achieve results. That's especially true if you're looking for hard data that (a) prove positive, sustainable change; and (b) can solidly attribute the change to the initiative. But the requests come—it's not a matter of *if*, but a matter of *when* you'll receive the challenge to prove, using data, your initiative's worth. I'm a firm believer in using data as a way of catching and sustaining the attention of initiative supporters. We'll talk, in detail, about data crises in a future chapter. For now, recognize that requests for data to justify an initiative investment are, at least in part, Attention Span Crisis driven.
No Public Relations (PR) Plan	
Initiative leaders must become part public relations professional in their work as they advocate for, and promote, their initiative's mere existence and, more critically, its impact. If you've not established and followed a plan for regularly promoting your accomplishments, setting and resetting expectations, and publicizing your impact, it's likely you and your initiative will eventually face the Attention Span Crisis.	

Strategies to Address the Attention Span Crisis

How do we catch and hold the attention of the people we need, that is, the people who will support our initiative? And, more challenging, how do we do that over time?

If you're reached the point of crisis, it's time to backtrack a bit and assess what you have, and haven't, done to promote your initiative within your school or district.

Here are the Attention Span Crisis tools that will support your way out of this crisis.

- Public Relations Blitz: Guidance for launching an initiative PR effort, including a planning tool for key messaging and evidence gathering

- Strategic Messaging: Priority approaches for sharing initiative information and accomplishments and getting it noticed

The example for these tools that follows comes from my own practice. Here is some background to inform your review of both the tools and the example I'll share in Figure 2. You can also view a full-color version and a collection of other examples at www.jamesmmarshall.com/projects.

Background for the Public Relations Blitz and Strategic Messaging Example

I have a long-standing initiative in Sexual Health Education led by an amazing program manager, Rachel Miller, for which I serve as evaluator to the San Diego Unified School District. With funding from the Centers for Disease Control and Prevention's (CDC) Division of Adolescent School Health (DASH), Rachel Miller leads a diverse effort to educate, build safe and supportive environments, and bolster sexual health services available to young people. In California, programs are guided by the California Healthy Youth Act (CHYA), which helpfully directs work in many of these areas. The initiative prioritized key areas of impact, all of which were benchmarked against CHYA's directive. Using a mix of collected data that address both implementation and outcomes, we chose to regularly update district leaders on our accomplishments. Additionally, our reporting was shared with CDC team members to quantify progress and demonstrate accomplishments against the CHYA-directed policy. The four-page piece we put together illustrates many of the strategic messaging elements I've encouraged you to apply to your PR-related efforts.

One additional note: The fact we are strategically using data to "prove" the key messages also makes this example an especially relevant solution for data-related crisis.

9. Public Relations Blitz

No one told you, upon taking up leadership of an initiative, that you had also just become a public relations (PR) agent. Well, that's a fact, and let me introduce you to your new client: your initiative.

It doesn't matter whether the initiative is school-based or districtwide, your PR work should promote key aspects of the effort to all. That should intentionally include those from whom you require support.

Whether PR is the heart of the crisis you face, or you're facing another primary crisis, most initiatives can do a better job promoting their existence, their progress, and their results. So, regardless of which situation you face, it is likely that a PR blitz should be part of your solution effort.

Your PR planning begins by defining the *who* and the *what*.

Audience	Key Message(s)
The Who	Step 1 is identifying the different people, or roles, to whom you must communicate. Later, you'll develop messaging for each, knowing that rarely does a single message communicate effectively to everyone you need to reach.
Primary Suspects	Top of your list are the people who are experiencing the Attention Span Crisis. The typical suspects here are the following: • Top-level district leadership • Board of education members • Second-level leaders (e.g., district financial officers, regional assistant superintendents) • Elected officials whose support is necessary • Funding organizations for initiatives that result from grant or foundation funding
Secondary Suspects	Second, expand your thinking to those who, in an ideal world, would know about your initiative's work and results. • For now, set aside topics of promoting the initiative to potential participants. • Focus on those whose support the initiative requires. Often, student-focused initiatives either rely on, or are fueled by, the support of parents. Thus, parents and families may be an audience for your PR campaign. I've often contributed to work that relied upon support from community partners.
The What	An initiative PR plan should lay out ongoing messaging over time and for each audience. • In doing so, you'd plan and then "feed" content to your audiences at key points in time. • From early messaging around the initiative's genesis, to launch, then early implementation-related updates, and eventually accomplishments and impact, you'd have sequenced communication and done so in a way that speaks to each of your key audiences.
Tactics	Since you're here because of crisis, we need to focus on the design of some immediate messaging. Still, think beyond that in your response, just so we avoid revisiting the crisis you currently face. I've provided a PR Blitz Campaign Planning tool for your use in designing this messaging. I've included a sample key message, which you'll note matches the example of PR headlines in action (Figure 2).

With the who and the what defined, turn your attention to messaging and producing a plan to deliver messages to the people who need to hear them. I suggest you define messages in three specific areas: (1) building general initiative awareness; (2) promoting accomplishments related to implementation progress —including early wins; and (3) promoting achievement of outcomes that demonstrate impact. Figure 2 offers an example from my practice that reflects public relations campaign planning and strategic messaging (our next strategy). The embedded example in the planner (below) is realized, in part, in Figure 2.

Audience	Key Message(s)	Evidence/Data to Support	Follow-up Plan
The people(s) or roles to which your messages will be directed	Headlines, in the form of sound bites, targeted to audience	Evidence you will use to substantiate each key message (where possible)	Plan for reinforcing the key messages beyond the initial sharing
Superintendent & Cabinet	• More schools are engaging parents in sexual health education. • We've reached the highest implementation levels, ever.	• Percentage of schools engaging parents over time (Profiles data)	• Update figures when available. • Press to share with Board of Education. • Follow up with complementary parent-focused evidence mid-year.
Raising Awareness: Messages related to the general initiative			
Implementation Accomplishments: Messages related to implementation progress			
Outcome and Impact: Messages related to the initiative's impact, typically based on defined outcomes			

10. Strategic Messaging

Message design is a critical element in realizing an effective PR plan. Your messaging may need to be responsive to the concern or question that launched you down this road to crisis resolution. Or, if you're operating proactively to avoid crisis, you can apply these principles to almost any messaging you'll produce. The ideas are particularly relevant to the reporting of data. Let's look at some common attributes that effective messages might share.

The example that follows (Figure 2) is something that I often use throughout an initiative's life cycle and it is designed to accomplish everything just described. As you review it, note the use of a headline and data to support the claim the headline makes. If all people do is review the headline and note the improved state reflected by the data, we could argue this PR effort is a success. And, in fact, that is exactly why it was designed, as you'll see.

Use this checklist to inform your thinking around strategic messaging and again to review and optimize your strategic messaging drafts.

	Strategy	Getting It Done
1	Think Headlines and Sound Bites	When an initiative is in an attention span crisis, make your messaging pithy. Use bullets to frame a handful of priority headlines to share. As you gain attention back, you can build upon the priority headlines in subsequent communications.
2	Level Your Messages	Give a headline that summarizes your key point and then offer a sentence or two of additional detail for those who seek it. Fun fact: I'm doing that right now between the left and right columns.
3	Make It a Must Read	Leveling the messaging provides for those who will only read the first phrase (e.g., the title in the left column here). But I like to play a game with myself where the challenge is to make that first phrase so enticing that people cannot help themselves from reading the supporting sentences that follow (e.g., the descriptions in this column).
4	Use Data for Persuasion	Data can make your messages both attention-riveting and convincing. Data are often seen as adding objectivity to the kinds of claims and assertions our initiative headlines must include. The Data Crisis section dives deep into finding data to support PR efforts and beyond.
5	Once Is Not Enough	Plan to reinforce your initial messaging by sending a complementary, follow-up message (or set of messages). Here, consider how you will reframe the initial headlines (rather than simply repeat them) and when the follow-up will occur.

People need a reason to invest time in reading, which is nicely proven by you picking up this book when compelled by initiative crisis! Often, the amount of information anyone is willing to read is driven, at least in part, by attaining and holding their interest. This is particularly true for overcommitted people, which undoubtedly includes some of the key audience members you're needing to reach.

How will you know you're on an effective track toward strategic messaging? Here are a handful of indicators:

- Challenge yourself to boil messages down, to use data that catch and maintain the reader's attention, and to eliminate unnecessary words and phrases.

- As you engage in this effort, if you find yourself revising and rewriting a few times, you're on the right track.

- When engaging in this work, I write, reflect, and then revise; walk away, reflect, revise; walk away, reflect, and then revise once again. It is the iterative reflection and revision that hone your message and increase its potential impact.

SAN DIEGO UNIFIED SCHOOL DISTRICT
Sexual Health Education Program | Leadership and Learning

2022 Profiles
Data Update

California Healthy Youth Act Implementation
An Analysis of School Accomplishments

The California Healthy Youth Act (CHYA), enacted January 1, 2016, requires school districts to provide comprehensive sexual health education and HIV prevention education to students in grades 7-12. The California Department of Education describes CHYA's five primary purposes as follows:

1. To provide pupils with the knowledge and skills necessary to protect their sexual and reproductive health from HIV and other sexually transmitted infections and from unintended pregnancy;
2. To provide pupils with the knowledge and skills they need to develop healthy attitudes concerning adolescent growth and development, body image, gender, sexual orientation, relationships, marriage, and family;
3. To promote understanding of sexuality as a normal part of human development;
4. To ensure pupils receive integrated, comprehensive, accurate, and unbiased sexual health and HIV prevention instruction and provide educators with clear tools and guidance to accomplish that end; and
5. To provide pupils with the knowledge and skills necessary to have healthy, positive, and safe relationships and behaviors.

While the San Diego Unified School District (SDUSD) had historically provided elements of this educational content, CHYA expanded the work and necessitated new efforts and curricular resources. Working with schools across the District as well as with community partners and public health experts, SDUSD's Sexual Health Education (SHE) Program team researched and recommended new curriculum that best aligned with CHYA requirements, which SDUSD's Board of Education adopted in July 2016. The team continues to oversee the program's implementation, which includes professional development for teachers to ensure they have the necessary content knowledge, as well as comfort and confidence to successfully deliver the curriculum.

Research conducted with Centers for Disease Control and Prevention (CDC) has provided insight into the evolution of the District's work over time. Using the biennial School Health Profiles data collection efforts, this document highlights the District's response to CHYA requirements that are aligned with SHE. These data are especially relevant because they provide a picture of school efforts before, during, and following the CHYA-required transition.

Profiles 2014	Profiles 2016	Profiles 2018	Profiles 2020	Profiles 2022
Surveys completed prior to CHYA	Surveys completed during the first year of CHYA-aligned curriculum implementation	Surveys completed during the third year of implementation	Surveys completed during the fifth year of implementation	Surveys completed during the seventh year of implementation

In addition, program evaluation conducted as part of CDC-funded District work offers an understanding of how District-provided professional development prepares participating teachers to deliver the curriculum.

School Health Profiles Survey

School Health Profiles (Profiles) is a system of surveys assessing school health policies and practices in states, large urban school districts, and territories.

Profiles data are collected from self-administered questionnaires from the principal and the lead health education teacher at each sampled school. The survey instruments allow these respondents to describe comprehensive aspects of their schools' work within the broad context of health.

Profiles places significant emphasis on assessing sexual health education efforts occurring in surveyed schools.

Key Findings

1. Almost All Schools are Engaging Parents in the Sexual Health Education of their Children

Percentage of Schools Engaging Parents through Homework Activities and Sexual Health Information

CHYA 6e: Instruction and materials shall encourage a pupil to communicate with his or her parents, guardians, and other trusted adults about human sexuality and provide the knowledge and skills necessary to do so.

Profiles Question: During this school year, have teachers in this school given students health education homework assignments or activities to do at home with their parents?

Profiles Question: During this school year, did your school provide parents and families with health information designed to increase parent and family knowledge of: HIV, other STD, or pregnancy prevention?

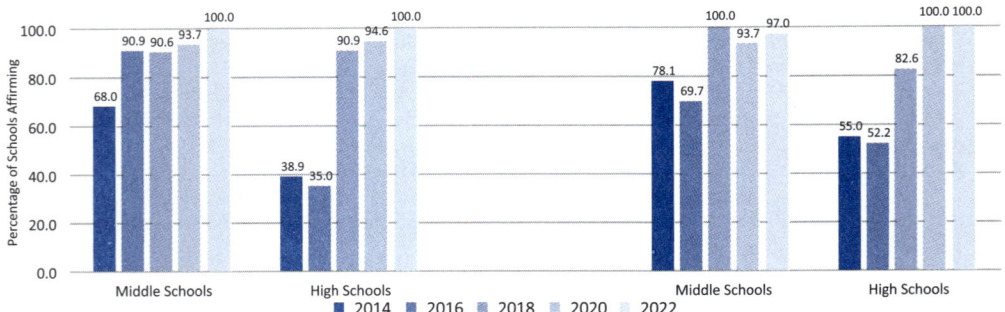

A comparison of Profiles results between 2014 and 2022 finds all schools implementing instruction and almost all providing materials—including homework—to engage parents in their child's sexual health education. By 2022, all middle schools were providing families with health information, and almost all middle and high schools were assigning sexual health education homework that involved parent-student communication about the topic. The regression for high schools between 2014 and 2016 coincides with the implementation of the District's new sexual health curriculum and most likely reflects the early transitions that schools experienced. More recent results signal close to full, districtwide implementation.

2. All Schools Now Teach Gender Roles, Identity, and Expression

Percentage of Schools Teaching Dimensions of Gender

CHYA 6: Instruction and materials shall teach pupils about gender, gender expression, gender identity, and explore the harm of negative gender stereotypes.

Profiles Question: During this school year, did teachers in your school teach the following sexual health topics in a required course for students: Gender roles, gender identity, gender expression?

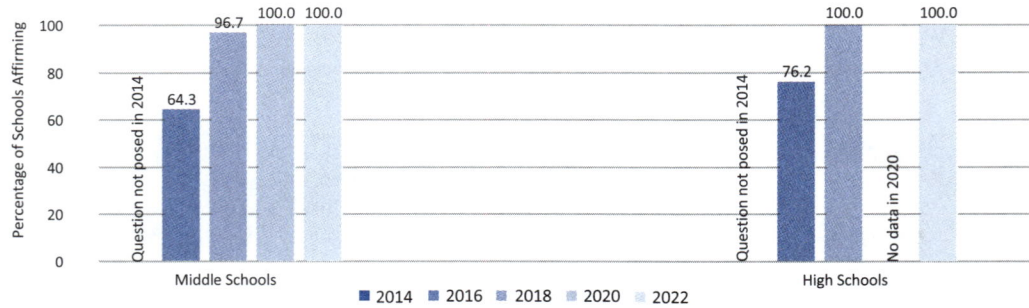

While not assessed before CHYA implementation began, a comparison of School Health Profiles responses from 2016 to 2022 illustrates dramatic growth in the use of instruction and materials that cover varied dimensions of gender. An additional 36% of middle schools achieved this outcome between 2016 and 2022. An additional 24% of high schools realized this outcome over the evaluation period. Today, a full 100% of middle and high schools are teaching gender roles, gender identity, and gender expression.

3. All Schools Now Provide Inclusive Instruction based on Diverse Dimensions of Identity
Percentage of Schools Implementing Inclusive Sexual Health Curricula

CHYA 1: Instruction and materials shall be appropriate for use with pupils of all races, genders, sexual orientations, and ethnic and cultural backgrounds, pupils with disabilities, and English learners.

Profiles Question: Does your school provide curricula or supplementary materials that include HIV, STD, or pregnancy prevention information that is relevant to lesbian, gay, bisexual, transgender, and questioning youth?

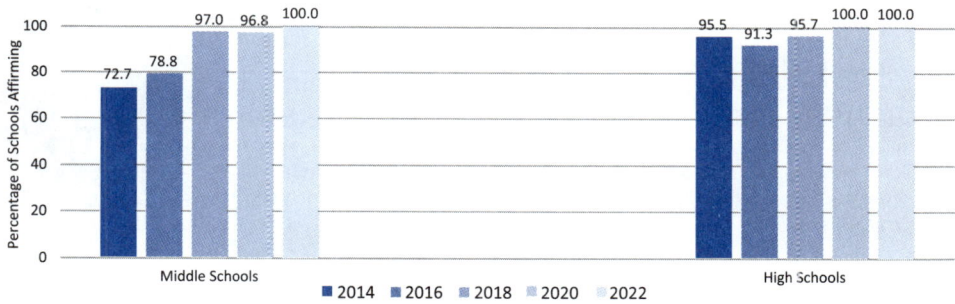

While almost all high schools have historically provided fully inclusive sexual health education instruction and materials, the same could not be previously said for middle schools. As a result of CHYA and the implementation of new, expansive curriculum, all middle and high schools now provide instruction and materials that are appropriate to use with people of all races, genders, sexual orientations, ethnic and cultural backgrounds, disabilities, and those learning English.

4. All Schools Now Use Materials that Include Diverse Sexual Orientations and Relationships
Percentage of Schools Using Materials that Cover Diverse Sexual Orientations

CHYA 5: Instruction and materials shall affirmatively recognize that people have different sexual orientations and, when discussing or providing examples of relationships or couples, shall be inclusive of same-sex relationships.

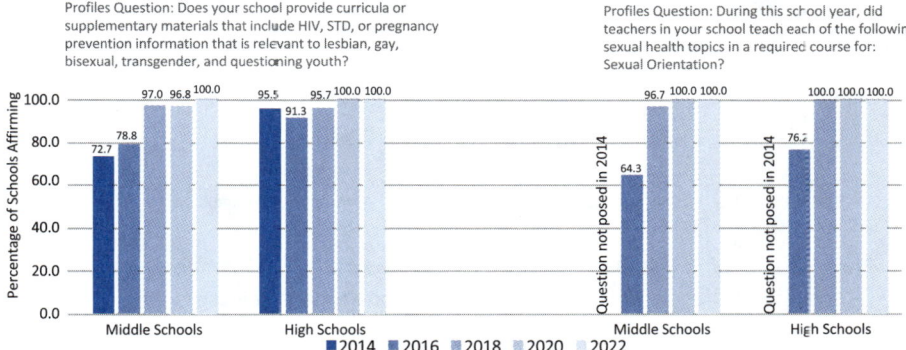

Our comparison of School Health Profiles responses between 2014 and 2022 also reveals a greater number of both middle and high schools now covering broad categories of sexual orientation. Today, 100% of middle and high schools implement curriculum relevant to LGBTQ youth. Additionally, 100% of middle and high schools are covering sexual orientation as part of their sexual health education program.

Teacher Professional Learning Supports these Accomplishments

Teachers have deemed the transition to, and implementation of, the CHYA-aligned curriculum a continued success. We attribute this success to the systematic curriculum selection and implementation process, of which professional development and implementation support are key components.

We assessed teachers prior to and following their SHE-focused professional development to measure changes in their self-assessed levels of content knowledge, competence, and comfort. While the post-professional development indicators reflected greater numbers of teachers self-assessing as competent, these skills would ultimately need to be applied in the classroom. We conducted an additional round of data collection to follow-up with teachers after their curriculum implementation.

Survey responses suggest increased levels of knowledge, competence, and comfort for teachers.

Response trends from over 200 implementing teachers, between 2016 and 2022, continue to indicate the successful implementation of the curriculum. Teachers indicate increased levels of knowledge, competence, and comfort. The following charts illustrate the distribution of teacher responses prior to and following the professional development sessions for a selected range of key indicators.

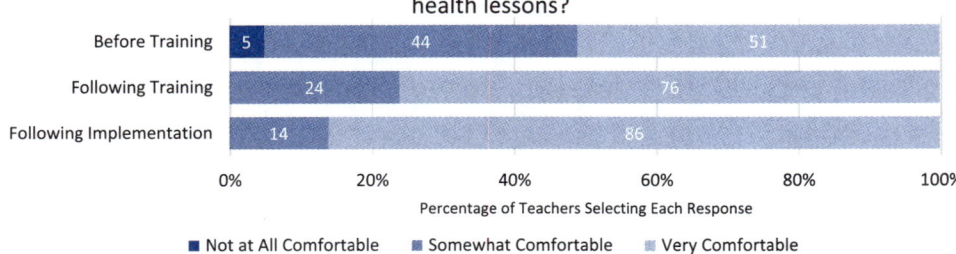

Question: How comfortable are you with teaching LGBT-inclusive sexual health lessons?

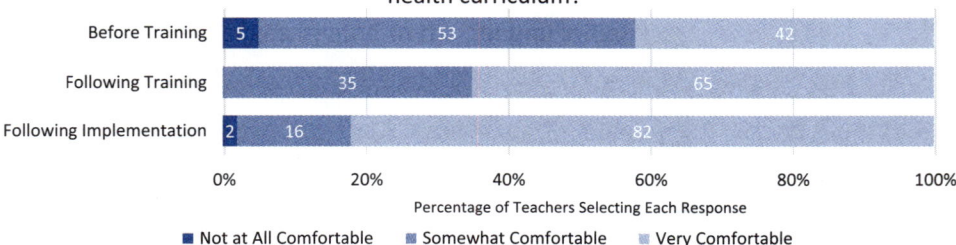

Question: How comfortable are you talking with parents about the sexual health curriculum?

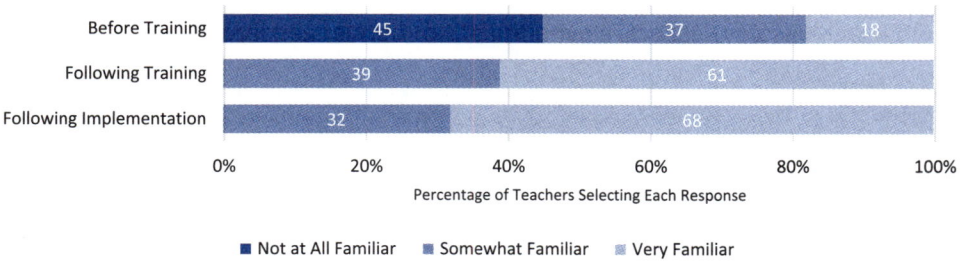

Question: How familiar are you with the facts regarding the CA Minor Consent Laws for Confidential Medical Care and Student Release?

Project Director: Rachel Miller, San Diego Unified School District   External Evaluator: James Marshall, Ph.D., San Diego State University

Data Crisis

We are mostly fortunate to live in a data-rich world. Educational leaders are increasingly surrounded by systems that we can consult in real time to understand many dimensions of teacher and student performance. Given the availability of data, it can be shocking when you realize you're leading an initiative with little or no data to justify its existence.

While numbers are my first love, I've come to, almost equally, appreciate the value of qualitative data in support of a true understanding of any given situation or scenario. I believe some data are better than none, as long as what you have is accurate and representative of what the data describe (think valid and reliable). In other words, don't make the inability to launch the randomized controlled study you may believe your initiative's evaluation requires the justification for doing nothing. Said more plainly, not being able to gain the data you believe to be "ideal" for your evaluation shouldn't justify pursuing the more accessible data that can inform your initiative's ongoing operation.

How do we know we're doing this right?

Are these results what we expected? Are they good enough? Couldn't they be better? Shouldn't they?

Can you prove that our investments in this program are actually delivering any sort of return for our teachers? Our students?

It's six months in, and what have we really accomplished?

Things aren't going well, but I have no idea what we should change to turn this thing around.

Is there any evidence this program even works?

Recognizing the Data Crisis

Data crises take multiple forms. At their core, they each involve not having the right data, at the right time, for the right purposes. Often, this results from data not getting the attention they deserve during the initiative's design.

Sometimes the data piece is like a can kicked down the road, with the more familiar initiative design tasks taking priority (e.g., designing the training, producing curriculum or other participant materials). Other times, when you find yourself shopping for a new initiative, step back to take stock of the initiatives around you. Then ask if they've been given the time they need to provide a (data-proven) return on the investment. If the answer is "not long enough," pursuing some data may be the best first step, before launching an entirely new initiative.

Let's define some typical data-related crises that impact initiatives (Table 5).

TABLE 5 Types of Data-Related Crises

Crisis	How You Know It
No Data to Guide Implementation	Well into the initiative's implementation, you begin to informally observe that things aren't going as well as you'd like. • You might see teacher resistance to the change the initiative requires. • More overtly, you find program resources stacked in a classroom cabinet, pristinely shrink-wrapped in their original state. • Or, rather than following the program's intended implementation plan, you walk in to find teachers and students doing the exact opposite. If you're not carefully monitoring the implementation by collecting regular feedback and documenting accomplishments that relate to *process,* sooner or later this is the situation you may very well face.
No Data to Sustain the Path to Impact	There are so many programs and initiatives out there that, at face value, seem like a perfect fit for our needs. • Yet, perhaps it is this *supply exceeds demand* disequilibrium that breeds commitment issues that are, in part, a data-related crisis. • Like the shiny new object that catches our attention, we leaders can be fickle as we jump from one program to the next, not giving our initial investment the time it needs to return results. When we collect formative data to describe the incremental accomplishments that are intended to add up to impact, we gain the confidence to "stay the course." The earliest and most limited pieces of evidence can provide what I term "promising evidence of future results."

TABLE 5 Types of Data-Related Crises *(Continued)*

Crisis	How You Know It
No Impact Data	When it comes to impact data, it isn't a matter of "if" but rather "when" you will be asked to justify your initiative's existence. • Sooner or later someone will question the investment. • "Is this program really making a difference?" "Is this the best use of our resources right now?" "Look over there at Program X—why isn't your program producing those kinds of results?" • Often, the person doing the questioning is not an educator; quite often such challenges come from the financial side of the organization. What might surprise you is that, in many cases we do find useable data that are already out there. Crisis results when we haven't made the effort to collect, use, and benefit from the data.
Not Great Impact Data	What happens when you have the impact data, but they aren't good? • You may face poor impact data early on in the program's implementation to the point where that poor impact data are argued as justification for the program's immediate elimination. • In such cases, the right thing to do might be to learn from the not-so-great data, in the spirit of continuous improvement and course correction. • Realize that it is not unusual for impact data collected early on in an initiative's lifecycle to not be everything we wished. Addressing this crisis will call upon your leadership skills in terms of evaluating the veracity of the data, and the difference between what you have and what you hoped to have at that point in time.
Too Much Data	Data crises happen even when there are data—*lots and lots* of data. What do you do with all that data? Where do you begin when your eyes are crossed by the data at hand? First, here's what <u>not</u> to do: Use the data all at once with any audience or constituency. Teams in data-rich situations do occasionally become paralyzed by where to begin. So too with data-dense reports shared with the expectation of cheers, only to find that some didn't even look at the thick report, while others simply didn't understand the complex tables and figures.

Strategies to Address the Lack of Data Crisis

Successful initiative design relies upon carefully defined data that are collected in the natural course of the initiative's implementation. Successful initiatives integrate opportunities to produce relevant data right into the initiative's design rather than fully relegating data to the program evaluation task.

Embrace the fact that your use and appreciation of initiative-related data can change and evolve, and expand and contract, over an initiative's life cycle. The goal is to be responsive. In an ideal scenario, the initiative's design intentionally involves and utilizes data each step of the way. At present, we're being responsive to crisis, possibly because we've not intentionally attended to data needs and opportunities. So let's get on with how to turn that around.

Here are the Data Crisis tools that will support your way out of this crisis.

- Baking Impact Data Into the Initiative: Guidance for embedding data into the natural process of initiative implementation to inform continuous improvement and demonstrate program impact

- Using the Evidence You Already Have: Where to look for existing information and data when evidence is demanded but program evaluation hasn't happened

- Pursuing Impact Evidence Over Time: Approach for gathering relevant impact evidence throughout the initiative's implementation cycle, from Day 1 forward

11. Baking Impact Data Into Your Initiative

Collecting data to describe an initiative's implementation and impact is often an afterthought. It's something that is done *to* the initiative rather than as *a part of* the initiative. But what if the data you required, even some of it, was generated organically, as a natural result of implementing the initiative?

Baking data into the initiative means finding ways to make data-generating activities, assessments, and evaluations a natural and symbiotic part of the initiative's implementation. In the natural course of, say, teachers running the program in their classrooms, we offer design elements that have the teachers documenting their implementation and students producing initiative-related artifacts that instantiate both implementation and impact. In these ways, the initiative itself is generating useful data simply by operating as designed.

Here are four reasons why the *baking* approach works.

	Reason	Rationale
1	Initiative participants implement and generate the data.	Instead of "the evaluator" giving a "test," program facilitators lead participants through exercises or other data-generating activities where they come to understand their own existing skill, knowledge, and performance levels. This can serve as a press for action —in the form of being motivated to learn and grow.
2	Early and ongoing program-generated data = ongoing needs assessment insight.	When used early on, the facilitators overseeing implementation gain needs assessment data that depict the current state of their participants, which then allows customizing and tailoring of the content they had planned to present, and the initiative overall.
3	Ongoing data, generated by the initiative, keep things on track, even if the track must shift.	With regular data collection occurring with the natural course of program implementation, leaders have the chance to see their participants' evolution over time. This supports the program's natural, data-based evolution to meet participant needs.
4	When collected and compiled over time, baked data directly supports the overarching program evaluation effort.	The body of evidence continues to naturally grow, in support of the initiative's ongoing evaluation, collection of data, and eventual investigation of defined, longer-term impacts. Results provide tangible, authentic evidence that serves the program evaluation requirement and demonstrates the program's impact on participants.

As you think about addressing your current crises, look for opportunities within the initiative itself for your implementers and participants to generate data that accomplish the following three things at the same time:

- Informs the successful implementation of the initiative (e.g., generates early data to help understand the participants' current state).
- Engages the participants in producing meaningful, program-aligned artifacts that result simply from their participation and engagement in the initiative.
- Provides useful evidence that can be used to describe the program's implementation and impact.

To illustrate the "baking content" fix, here's an example from my own practice that proved successful some years ago. The following context will inform your review of the example that follows.

Background for the Concept Map Example

I served as program evaluator for many years on a U.S. Department of Education–funded Teaching American History grant program. Led by Laurie Mosier, a consortium of districts was funded to the tune of five million dollars to increase the content knowledge and pedagogy of middle and high school U.S. history teachers. As evaluator, and over the course of the five-year project, my job was to document the program's implementation and demonstrate its impact. Naturally, that involved measuring teacher content knowledge. To do that, we needed to establish the teachers' baseline knowledge as they entered the program.

Instead of giving them the expected test of U.S. history knowledge, we tried something different. Knowing the rightly narrow scope of U.S. history on which our project's leadership intended to focus, our team developed a concept mapping activity that the teachers completed on their first day. Working from a starter "node" in the concept map, it challenged teachers to elaborate their subject matter knowledge specific to the core content. In doing so, we recorded their existing knowledge in both breadth and depth. The theory was that as they participated in the program, their subject matter knowledge would deepen. Then, when we repeated the concept mapping activity at the program's conclusion, we anticipated—if successful—we would find greater and more sophisticated elaborations.

Our example includes the concept mapping exercise description, along with a pre- and post-initiative concept map from the same middle school teacher-participant. We also developed a rubric to turn the concept map performance into quantified data for pre to post comparisons (e.g., number of accurate vs. inaccurate concepts, number, and depth of connections) (Figures 3–5).

FIGURE 3   Concept Mapping Exercise Used Pre- and Post-participation

Concept Mapping Exercise

Concept Maps are an effective tool for presenting your understanding of a given topic or idea. As we begin and conclude our learning study cycles, we will dedicate 15 minutes to concept mapping your current understanding of the selected content area.

Defining Features of Concept Maps

Concept Maps share two basic features:

1. **Concept Maps are hierarchical.**

   In general, they move from the more broad concepts (top) to the most specific concepts (bottom).

2. **Links include meaningful labels.**

   They describe how you connect the ideas in your mind.

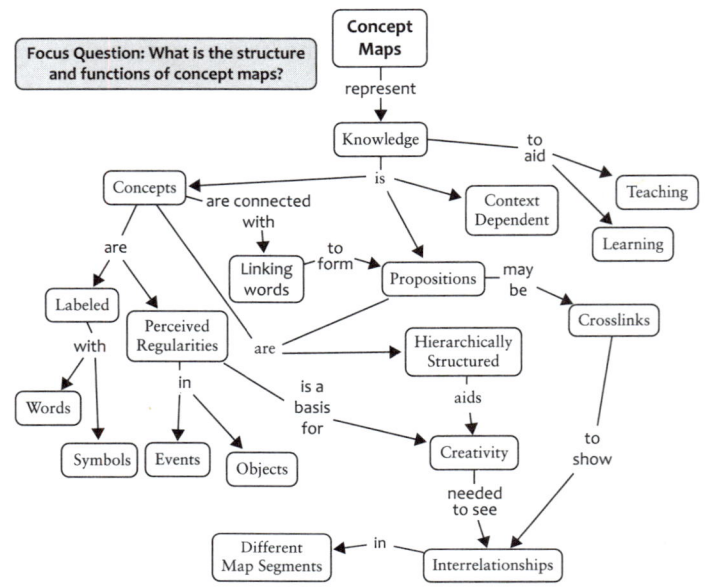

Review the adjacent *Concept Map of Concept Maps* (Novak, 1998, p. 36) and identify these two defining features.

Constructing a Concept Map: The Basics

1. List the concepts the given topic involves.
2. Rank concepts from most general; consider relationships in your rankings.
3. Arrange hierarchically on the page.
4. Add links and phrases that describe the relationships.
5. Review and revise: Does the concept map represent the **range of content** and the **organization of content** in your mind?

Today's Task

Using the topic generated by your group and your current understanding of that topic, construct a concept map on the back of this page. Your map should include the concepts involved in this topic and the relationships among those concepts.

FIGURE 4 • Concept Mapping Exercise Example—Pre-initiative

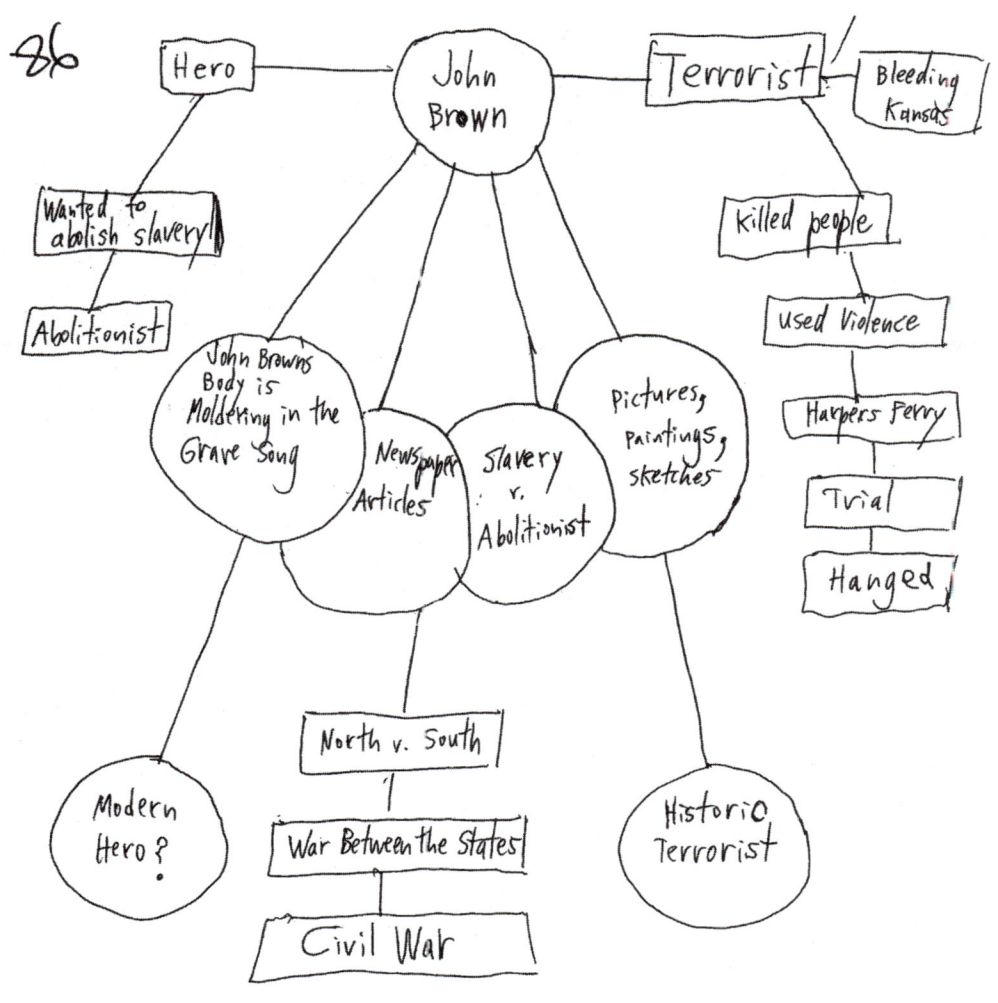

FIGURE 5 Concept Mapping Exercise Example—Post-initiative

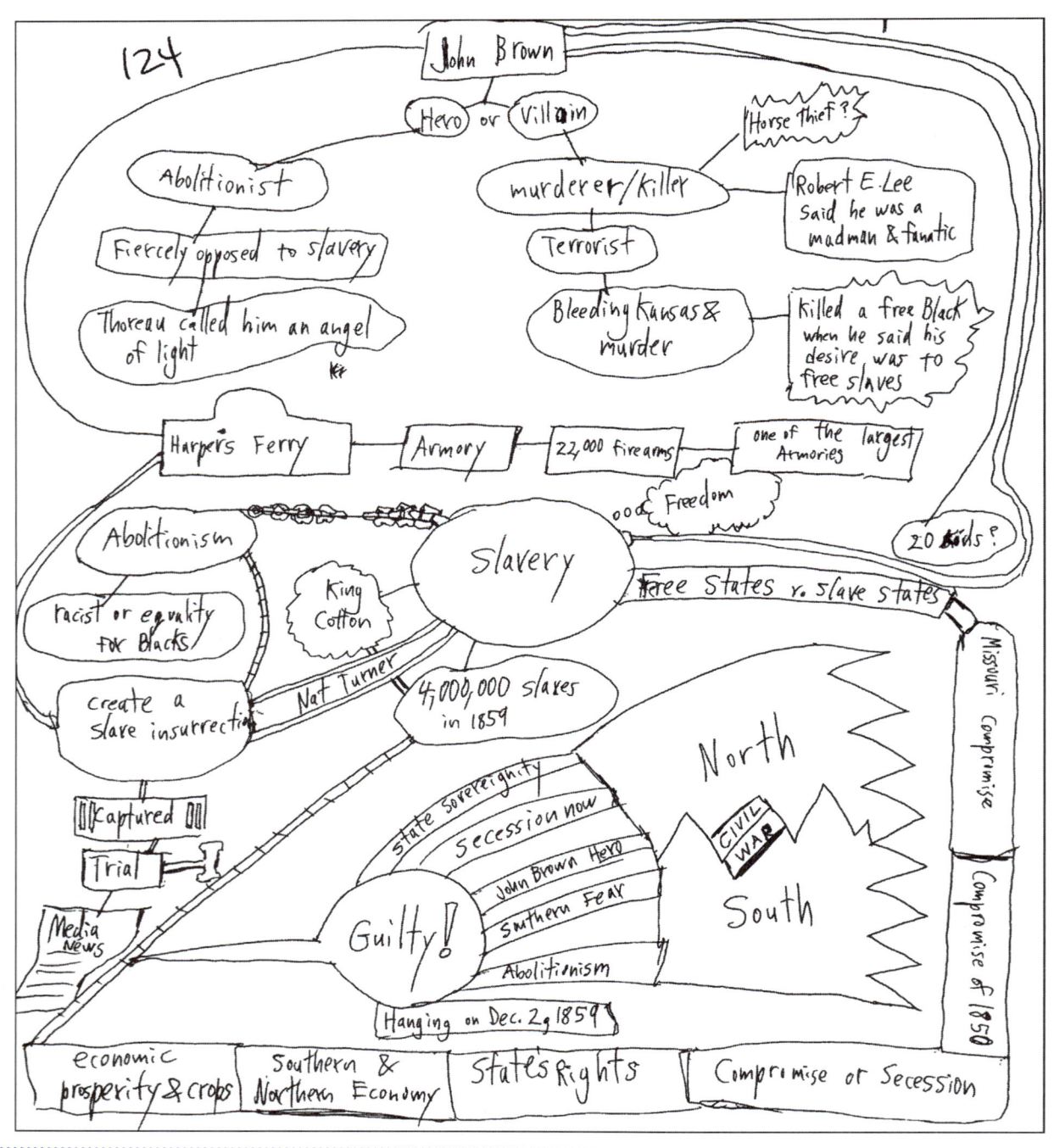

12. Using the Evidence You Already Have

What do you do when you haven't been collecting, let alone planning, to have the necessary data that "prove" an initiative's worth?

Certainly, this type of crisis usually points to the need for an evaluation plan if you've not already produced one. But when it comes to immediate action, one strategy is to go on a hunt for anything and everything you already have (or can quickly have) that can speak to the initiative's implementation and impact. What you're looking for is **evidence pockets**, that is, data related to your initiative, in some reasonable way, that already exist somewhere. Evidence pockets often aren't top-of-mind. They usually require brainstorming and creative thinking to identify. That makes sense; otherwise, they'd already be in use!

A fancy way to phrase all this is that we'll employ all the **extant data** we can find to support a review and documentation of the initiative's progress and impact. We may also choose to do some **just-in-time data collection,** as long as it can happen fast. Then we'll disseminate that evidence accurately, broadly, and persuasively (see page 47 for strategies addressing use of data in public relations efforts).

Use the following tool to identify a range of evidence that might support the current, crisis-induced data need.

Extant Data from Early Wins: A Powerful Combination

It's important to note that any Early Wins you've defined nicely intersect with the extant data strategy. When you define early wins, you automatically have a measurable piece of evidence that you can use to illustrate your initiative's forward momentum in the earliest stages. Thus, one way to employ this "leveraging what you already have strategy" is to summarize the evidence of achieved early wins. For example, if one early win was to train every teacher at your school on an initial set of social-emotional learning strategies, you can easily document that having happened. That training, in preparation for classroom implementation, offers evidence of the program's early implementation.

To illustrate the use of existing data, as well as data that are quick and easy to collect, here's an example from another past project led by the accomplished Utah Education Network chief operating officer and my colleague, Laura Hunter. This information will help you understand the examples that follow. You can view a full-color version of the report and a collection of other examples at www.jamesmmarshall.com/projects.

This checklist is designed to guide you in a review of high-potential sources of evidence that may already exist. Read through each possible evidence touchstone, consider that which you currently have access, and anything else that could be *quickly* and *efficiently* collected to expand your immediate evidence base.

	Potential Evidence	Description	Your Plan: Evidence Pockets and Just-in-Time Data Collection
1	Program Design	A Theory of Action or Logic Model that clearly defines the initiative and the logic behind the impact it is designed to achieve	
2	**Implementation-Related**		
2a	Outputs	Outputs you defined as part of the logic model that "prove" successful initiative implementation	
2b	Participation	Figures that quantify participation of leaders, implementers, participants, and any other involved constituency	
2c	Early Wins	Evidence produced as a result of achieving each defined early win	
2d	Implementation Artifacts	Anything generated by initiative participants that demonstrates initiative-related outcomes; e.g., teacher lesson plans on newly trained pedagogy and student work produced as part of the initiative	
3	**Impact-Related**		
3a	Participant Perspectives Describing the Initiative's Potential	Early on, some of the most powerful perspectives may come from those participating in your initiative. Collect and share the observations of those implementing the initiative and those who are participants. Informal interviews and testimonials are two examples of participant perspectives that can be collected on a just-in-time sort of timeline. An example from the UtahFutures program is included here.	

	Potential Evidence	Description	Your Plan: Evidence Pockets and Just-in-Time Data Collection
3b	Early, Promising Results	Evidence that can connect to the overarching impact, or a defined outcome, of your initiative. Early on, these can be relatively small indicators that suggest the initiative is on the right track to achieve its outcomes, for example, local achievement measures as early results on the road to more significant impact evidence (e.g., state or national tests). I offer an additional example (Lightspan) of this practice in the next strategy you'll read.	
3c	ABC (Already Being Collected) Data	Review the range of measures that are already being collected in your school or district. From teacher-generated data, to class assignments, attendance records, culture and climate surveys, parent engagement, there really is no shortage of data out there. Look for things that intersect with your initiative and work to build the association as indicators of progress.	

Background on the Participant Perspectives and Implementation Outputs Examples

As part of an effort to build evidence around the statewide implementation of the UtahFutures initiative to support college and career readiness, we solicited some just-in-time perspectives from the folks who implemented and used the online program (Utah Education Network, 2017). This was accomplished in a matter of days and provided some persuasive evidence, early on, about how the program was being used and the impact people were seeing in schools across the state. Figure 6 offers an example of our targeted request for feedback and the type of data that resulted.

Another example of using existing data to demonstrate initiative progress involves implementation-related data (see Figure 7). Part of our strategy for the same initiative used existing data that quantified the program's promotion and implementation across the state—which was carefully aligned to the Theory of Action's language that originally defined these approaches. As you review Figure 7, pay particular attention to the use of numbers that quantify an effort over less than two years to raise awareness and increase program use. These extant data provided a successful, while relatively early, indicator of the initiative's implementation efforts.

FIGURE 6 UtahFutures Just-in-Time Participant Perspectives Example

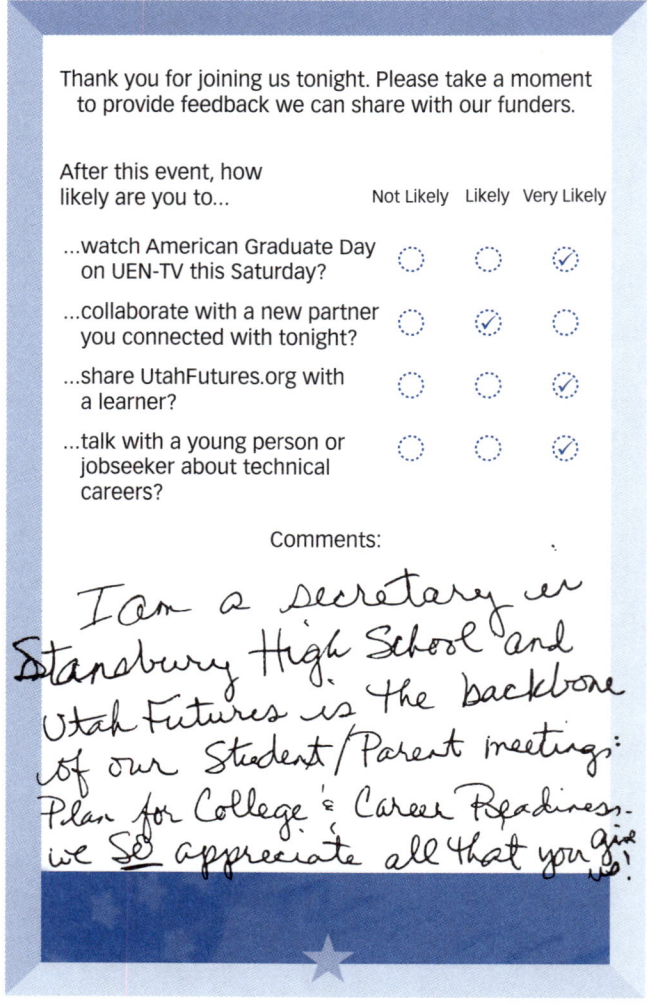

SOURCE: UEN.

FIGURE 7 UtahFutures Implementation Outputs Example

CROSS-STATE PROMOTION AND AWARENESS BUILDING:

UTAHFUTURES IS DISSEMINATED

IF YOU BUILD IT, will they come? Getting the word out about UtahFutures and the resources it provides is an ongoing effort for UETN. Of the organizations that provided a home for UtahFutures over the years, UETN is best equipped to carry out this critical element of the program's implementation. Statewide public broadcasting reach, an established professional development structure, governance representing a broad constituent base, and UETN's unique role as a technology provider across the state make UETN the right home for UtahFutures.

> **Statewide public broadcasting reach, an established professional development structure, governance representing a broad constituent base, and UETN's unique role as a technology provider across the state make UETN the right home for UtahFutures.**

How is UETN promoting the UtahFutures program to residents across the state?

UETN is currently engaged in disseminating UtahFutures through an intentionally diverse complement of strategies, with considerable reach.

UTAHFUTURES DISSEMINATION 2015-2017 BY THE NUMBERS

312	Hours of UtahFutures career education programs aired on KUEN
59	UtahFutures promotional spots aired on KUEN
949,000	Households in the KUEN viewing area
276,600	UtahFutures social media impressions
223	UtahFutures training sessions held statewide
4,931	School counselors and advisors trained by UtahFutures
7,000+	UtahFutures collateral pieces distributed during college application events
263	UtahFutures monthly newsletter subscribers

SOURCE: UEN.

13. Pursuing Impact Evidence Over Time

Initiatives take time: to plan, to implement, and to yield results. When carefully planned, we can collect evidence of impact each step of the way. So often, evaluating our programs becomes an afterthought. It is often something done *to* programs near their end. While summative evaluation has an important role in any initiative investment, there are opportunities to collect evidence each step of the way. Put plainly, you're not likely to have persuasive impact data a few months into implementation. But that doesn't mean you wait until the end to plan and pursue evidence.

Take note: Evidence is all around us and is present even in the earliest phases of implementation. Let me illustrate, by example, how successful initiative managers match their evidence collecting to different phases of an initiative's implementation to demonstrate this strategy in action.

Pursuing Impact Evidence Over Time Checklist

Here is a checklist to guide your thinking about the evolution and availability of evidence over the course of your initiative's implementation. It highlights where to look formatively and summatively, with the goal of having evidence each point along the way to (a) help you understand and continuously improve your initiative, and (b) regularly update your participants and supporters about your accomplishments and impact.

	Evidence	Where to Look	Suggestions
1	Take Early Steps, Using Early Wins	If you've defined early wins, it's likely that their achievement offers some of your earliest evidence of impact or promising steps forward on the way to impact.	• Use your early win data to celebrate progress with your team and participants. • Share early win data broadly to remind people of your initiative and demonstrate its successful early implementation and impact.
2	Promote Implementation Milestones	As you continue to implement, document your feats. Think about the number of people reached, the number of lessons taught, attendance and participation figures, engagement levels, etc. Each of these milestones can demonstrate your ongoing, forward momentum on the way to measurable impact.	• Share your implementation milestones broad and wide. • Early on, your story may be framed around implementation and participation. Challenge yourself to make connections between participation-related figures and the longer-term outcomes you're ultimately working toward. • For example, build a connection between consistent participation or attendance and the eventual outcome you seek.
3	Share Early Indicators of Promising Results	Be on the lookout for anything and everything that might signal you're on the right track. Listen for provocative statements made by participants that make you think, "Wow, they're really getting it!" or, "They're really into this," or "They've really begun to change." Also watch for even isolated cases of positive impact for some of your participants. Interrogate anything you see and hear to understand and, potentially add to your growing body of evidence.	• Often, the first true evidence of impact is heard casually, in passing. A student, a parent, or even a colleague says something about your initiative, typically out of the blue. Hearing how a struggling student has been buoyed by the program, or a reluctant learner has found true engagement with your novel initiative, are just two examples of how that might happen. • Even the smallest, positive development can be a promising result that is worth documenting and sharing. Profile the students in your program update, perhaps. Share perspectives from teachers about what they've observed, and what they believe it will meant impact wise and in the long term.

	Evidence	Where to Look	Suggestions
4	Collect and Share Foundational Indicators of Impact: The Building Blocks of Impact	As your implementation matures, think about the antecedents to your ultimate and deepest impact. Consult your logic model for observable and measurable components that, together and eventually, lead to the long-term impact you seek. And then work to measure these foundational indicators of impact.	• Impact doesn't happen overnight. When it comes to learning, we educators know true growth happens over time. But when we look closely, we typically can find discrete evidence of progress at most points along the process. • At this stage, you're looking for discrete indicators that realistically contribute to your targeted long-term impact. Think of them as the building blocks that, together, will provide the means to reach the desired impact. • Now's the time to identify them, find them, measure them, and report them to any all who will listen. Doing so demonstrates the high quality of your project and its implementation, while also providing data to inform necessary course adjustments and corrections.
5	Prove the Initiative's Ultimate Impact	Eventually your initiative will reach a reasonable degree of implementation. This is the point where longer-term impact can be assessed and reported. Be ready for this, and all previous steps, by producing an evidence or evaluation plan that guides what data you will collect and use at each point.	• Impact measures should be designed in a logic model. The mid- and long-term impacts are what you're now pursuing. • Measure impacts from multiple dimensions, whenever possible. For example, multiple measures of achievement in a learning-related initiative. • Then, use all the evidence you've collected this far to tell the full story. Connect your early win and early indicator data to the impact data you've documented. Integrate foundational indicators by using them as the logical pathway that leads toward the impact data you'll present. • Success here demonstrates the association between the initiative and the result, clearly showing the initiative's value in bringing about the better state you have now described.

This checklist has provided some categories, detail, and examples of evidence in five categories. Since we're "building" evidence, let's use building blocks as an analogy, given the fact that with each piece of useful and accurate data we're adding to the story that describes our initiative's implementation and impact.

As we practice this at each stage, we slowly develop a significant and solid structure of evidence about the initiative and the clear relationships among its design, implementation, and impact. The ultimate measures of impact rest at the top not only because they take time to achieve but also because they're fully supported by each of the other implementation- and impact-related early findings.

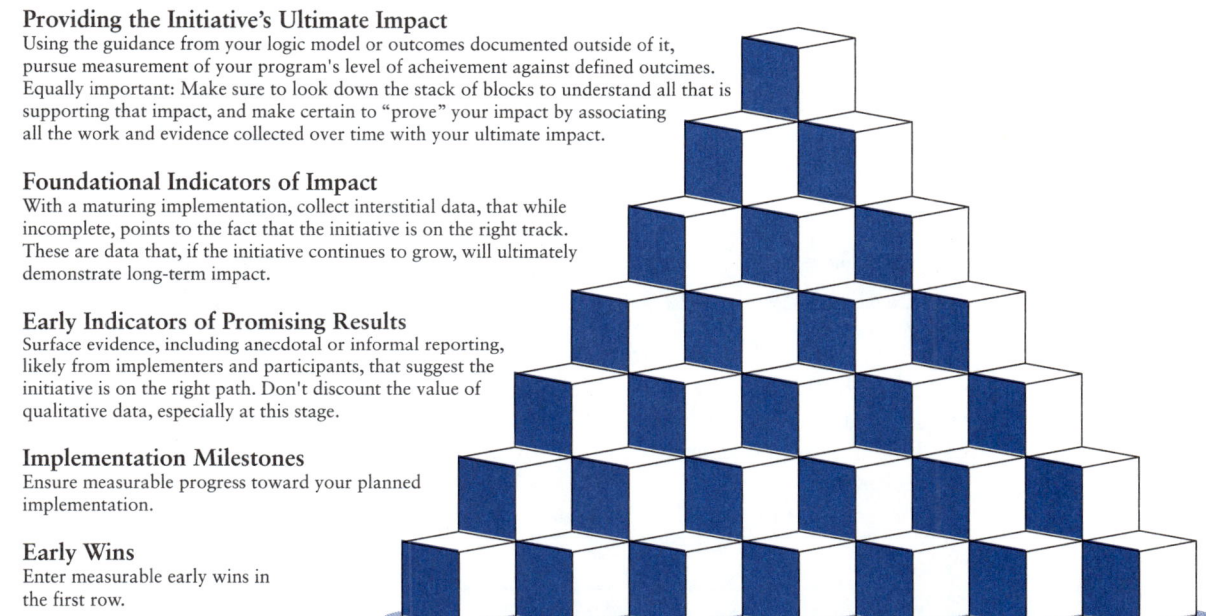

Providing the Initiative's Ultimate Impact
Using the guidance from your logic model or outcomes documented outside of it, pursue measurement of your program's level of acheivement against defined outcomes. Equally important: Make sure to look down the stack of blocks to understand all that is supporting that impact, and make certain to "prove" your impact by associating all the work and evidence collected over time with your ultimate impact.

Foundational Indicators of Impact
With a maturing implementation, collect interstitial data, that while incomplete, points to the fact that the initiative is on the right track. These are data that, if the initiative continues to grow, will ultimately demonstrate long-term impact.

Early Indicators of Promising Results
Surface evidence, including anecdotal or informal reporting, likely from implementers and participants, that suggest the initiative is on the right path. Don't discount the value of qualitative data, especially at this stage.

Implementation Milestones
Ensure measurable progress toward your planned implementation.

Early Wins
Enter measurable early wins in the first row.

I have the perfect example to share when it comes to using the data you have, or can have, at each stage of an initiative's implementation. It's important to remember that impact data takes time—first to become available and, thereafter, to collect, analyze, and disseminate. The example shows how that can be done with available data each step of the way, right up to the point of realizing your ultimate impact. Here's some background information that will help you understand the example that follows.

Background on the Lightspan Early Evidence Example

In the 1990s, I worked for a company that offered reading/language arts and mathematics curriculum to schools and districts that could be used in and out of schools with the goal of increasing student achievement. Long before the one-on-one laptop or Chromebook programs became prominent, Lightspan's novel program emerged at a time when the technology divide was notably present in Title I schools.

The formula for success was simple and evidence based. Table 6 is a re-creation of the formula that drove the work in a theory of action format.

TABLE 6 Lightspan's Theory of Action

Time + Family + Equity + Motivation = Student Achievement
If we:
• Increase the amount of **time** spent learning through technology in the home   • Increase the involvement of **families** in their children's education   • Increase **equitable access** so that all students have the ability to learn through technology   • Increase the **motivation** of children to not only learn but love to learn
Then:
• Students will engage in learning after school.   • Families will be more aware and engaged in their children's education.   • The digital divide will become a thing of the past.   • Children will develop a love of learning and choose to engage in their schoolwork.
Which will result in:
Increased achievement for all students in reading/language arts and mathematics

As the first programs were implemented in schools across the country, there was more than one school board that questioned the cost and the rather unorthodox approach of a PlayStation-run curriculum. Naturally, it would take time to establish the connection between Lightspan's program and high-stakes student achievement. Working with Lightspan's co-founder Bernice Stafford, we realized every other element behind the program's design could be measured right from the start (see Table 7). So we immediately began pre- and post-surveying parents and teachers after only a short time.

TABLE 7 Lightspan's Phased Data Collection Path to Impact

Area	Time + Family + Equity + Motivation = Achievement				
Key Question	Does the **time** dedicated to "learning" at home increase once Lightspan is sent home?	Do **families** have more interaction with their child's teacher?	Does the program provide **equitable access** to **all** students?	Do parents and teachers judge the students' **motivation** for learning to increase through program use?	Do students using Lightspan realize greater gains than a matched comparison group of non-users?
Key Measures	Pre-Post Surveys From Parents and Teachers	Pre-Post Parent Survey	Program Access Records	Pre-Post Surveys From Parents and Teachers	Locally Defined Achievement Measures (Typically State Test)
Collected	Formative Evaluation Collected following the initial implementation of the first program components going home with students				Summative Evaluation Measured following full initiative implementation

These were the areas in which we invested our earliest evaluation resources, after eight weeks of implementation, to offer teachers and schools a data-based early win for their program implementation accomplishments. If these things were indeed happening and the research had already proven that each contributed significantly to student achievement, then there had to be a positive, student achievement impact developing as teachers integrated the curriculum into their practice and students continued to use the program. And, in time with full and mature program implementation, that is exactly the student achievement impact we were able to prove.

When Things Don't Go as Planned (D-GAP) Crisis

Implementing programs is neither easy nor fast. For that reason, there are significant opportunities for things to not go as planned. Dedicated, intentional planning plus a systematic and systemic implementation approach contribute to your chances for the predictable results you seek. Yet even the best-laid, most data-informed initiative designs can face stormy weather when the "program meets world." When things don't go as planned and implementation stalls, you're typically facing situations and barriers you didn't expect. These causes fall into the "When things don't go as planned" crisis (let's call it *D-GAP* for short).

Well, I didn't see that coming!

I wasn't expecting to have to involve all these other people in our program.

How are we ever going to get our teachers to implement this program the way we designed it?

I guess "set it and forget it" doesn't apply here.

Our program is basically synonymous with [insert name], and they're leaving. Now what?

I keep hearing, "Why even bother?" People seem to think running this initiative is optional!

Recognizing a D-GAP Crisis

It would take far more pages than the number available here to cover all the different ways initiatives achieve a D-GAP crisis. Here are those most frequently encountered in my course of implementing and evaluating a diverse set of initiatives over more than 20 years' time (Table 8).

TABLE 8 Oft-Encountered D-GAP Crises

D-GAP Crises	Description
Floundering Fidelity	**Fidelity** flounders when the initiative's implementation deviates from the one you've carefully defined and matched to achieve the envisioned outcomes. When this happens, there may be multiple causes at play. From a lack of access to necessary resources, to a lack of understanding the "why" behind implementation as planned, many things can cause fidelity to go unachieved. Fidelity will flounder when expectations are unclear to those responsible for implementation.
As the Initiative Turns	The only thing about change is that it is inevitable. Initiatives require change and, typically, the change that initiatives require *changes*. Profound? Perhaps, but it's the reality faced by those who design and implement initiatives. While pursuing fidelity is critical, we must also provide for evolution and continuous improvement as part of the implementation adventure any initiative involves. The initiative will turn and our role, as leaders, is to be discerning about the fine line between being informed, but not imprisoned, by our original plan.
Smart Successions	It is not a matter of if, but rather when, those leading an initiative will transition to new pursuits. Changes in leadership at any level—from those running the initiative to the higher-ups supporting the initiative—can quickly cause things to deviate from what was planned. Being ready when this inevitably occurs is key to sustaining an initiative's impact.
Programitis	With the suffix -*itis* denoting inflammation, **programitis** describes an inflammation of programs within a school or district. It can result when new, additional programs are regularly introduced without consideration of those already in place. What follows is the piling on of new and additional programs. Programitis relates to multiple crises, but is typically uncovered as a cause when you realize things aren't going as planned.
I Don't Know How	Essentially, this is the pleading of ignorance that emanates from those responsible for initiative implementation. This can stem from a lack of training or guidance to support proper (fidelitous) implementation. It can also be prompted by a fear of failure—or even a fear of achieving anything less than complete success. Note that it is also not limited to those implementing the initiative. Participants too can stall in their initiative engagement because of not knowing how, or thinking they don't know enough to be successful.

TABLE 8 Oft-Encountered D-GAP Crises *(Continued)*

D-GAP Crises	Description
I Don't Wanna	Initiatives require change—for implementer and participant alike. When you haven't attended to managing the change that every initiative naturally requires, you'll likely experience push back, or the "I don't wanna."
I Don't Care/No One Cares	One simple reason for things not going as planned is a belief that the initiative and its success simply doesn't matter. Ask yourself, are there consequences if the initiative isn't implemented? For example, what happens when the new curriculum is left on the bookshelf in the back of the room? Better—what reward or recognition is in place when even the smallest accomplishment in the change process is realized? If your answers come up short, you're likely facing a "no one cares"–based D-GAP.

Here's a quick observation about the final three items on this list: When it comes to adults, you're less likely to hear them admit they don't know how. Our nature is such that we tend to avoid admitting what we don't know, even when we literally don't know how. Instead, we slough it off as having no value for us: "Meh, that's fine for you, but it's not my thing," or "No one really cares about this." In my experience, younger people are far more likely to admit they truly don't know how. The lesson: Take time to really understand what's behind the barrier you're facing.

Strategies to Address the D-GAP Crisis

Admittedly, almost any of the other crises in this book can lead to a D-GAP crisis. Successful initiatives operate as a system, while almost always existing within a system. When any element of our initiative system falters, it can quickly lead to things not going as planned. The strategies that follow are designed to address the unexpected things that crop up in the midst of implementation. But, could you suddenly face an outcomes crisis at the same point? Yes—and if you do, proceed to the relevant strategies. So too for the other crises categories I've shared.

Here are the D-GAP tools that will support your way out of this crisis.

- Making Human Performance Happen: Applying what the research says about human performance to identify root causes of flawed initiatives and to create environments where initiatives thrive

- Fidelity Check-up: Reviewing, or defining, your initiative's fidelity expectations and adjusting as necessary

- Backing Your Way Into the Perfect Solution: A strategic approach for brainstorming the "ideal" initiative, informed by data you've collected, and then working your way back to something that matches your available resources

- Early Wins: Strategy for defining early initiative milestones and leveraging them to give your initiative forward momentum

- Navigating the White Space: Tips for gaining and sustaining buy-in by following your organization chart—what's written and what happens between the boxes

14. Making Human Performance Happen

Human performance technology (HPT) stems from the field of **behavioral engineering** where the early, biggest thinker was, arguably, Thomas Gilbert (2007). Over the decades, HPT has been applied, observed, modified, and honed. Among those who have influenced the field, and whose ideas are incorporated into what you'll read here, are Robert Mager and Peter Pipe (1997), Harold Stolovitch and Erica Keeps (1992), Geary Rummler and Alan Brache (1996), and Allison Rossett (2009). It is Rossett's work, in particular, that has influenced my own understanding and evolution of thought when it comes to what drives human performance.

The human performance drivers are predicated on the fact that for anyone to be successful these are the things that *need* to be present. Some reside within the individual who is doing the performing, whereas the others are things that must be provided by the organization. Here are some of the queries typically used to triage D-GAPs, build our initial understanding, and inform our next steps toward solutions. At the risk of sounding like a fanatic, they are magical in terms of the clarity they bring to our thinking. And let's face it: When you're dealing with a crisis, it is very easy to become overwhelmed and find yourself waffling about, lacking commitment to a solid course of action you will take.

You'll note they're referenced as both *barriers* to and *drivers* of performance. When they aren't present, they serve as barriers. But when they *are* present, as they should be, they serve to drive someone's performance toward the ideal outcome.

The following checklist describes each category and offers some relevant examples to help you picture the barrier/driver in action.

Barrier	Driver Category	Description	Examples
Inside the Individual		
Knowledge and Skill	Possessing the necessary information, and having sufficient opportunity to practice, to influence successful performance	• Adequate training that also supports application of trained skills, over time, on the job • Opportunity to practice and perfect involved performance • Access to supports that target knowledge and skill, including coaching and reference guides
Motivation	Value × Confidence = Motivation In other words, motivation is the product (think multiplication) of value and confidence. Just like any number multiplied by zero is zero, when either is absent (zero), overall motivation is reduced or eliminated.	
Value	The import one ascribes to performing	• Personal dedication to performing • Held beliefs that performance will make a positive difference
Confidence	The beliefs one holds about whether one will, or won't, be successful	• Measures of self-efficacy • Held assumptions about whether one is capable of performing and the degree to which one will succeed if an attempt is made
Driven by the Organization		
Incentives	Things the organization offers that reward successful performance	• Anything that the organization provides that signals a positive reinforcement for performance • Often thought of as pay for performance, money • Can be as simple as providing feedback • This category also includes punitive measures as consequences for non-performance
Environment	Comprised of Tools, Expectations, and Time	
Tools	Ready access to the tools and resources required for successful performance	• Computers, programs, subscriptions • Curriculum-required elements, like manipulatives • References that can guide performance while it occurs
Expectations	Clear expectations, sometimes through policy, that align with successful performance	• Directives that prioritize performance • Policy that doesn't contradict performance
Time	Time required to perform is made available	• The realistic and necessary time commitment is recognized and acknowledged • Competing priorities are adjusted such that necessary time is available

With an understanding of the different categories, here are some questions you can use to explore the influence of each barrier/driver within the context of your initiative's crisis.

Barrier | Driver Category	Description	Triage Questions
Inside the Individual		
Knowledge and Skill	Possessing the necessary information, and having sufficient opportunity to practice, to influence successful performance	• If their lives depended on performing, could they do it? • What training has been provided? • What supports are in place to ensure successful performance? • What involved knowledge or skill have we (a) seen performed with success, (b) not seen performed, and (c) seen performed *without* success?
Motivation	Value × Confidence = Motivation	
Value	The import one ascribes to performing	• Do they understand the "why" behind performing? • How would they describe the reasons performance is important? • What evidence do we have that performance matters to them, personally?
Confidence	The beliefs one holds about whether one will, or won't, be successful	• What level of confidence do they have in performing? • What evidence do we have that concerns about failing may be getting in the way?
Driven by the Organization		
Incentives	Things the organization offers that reward successful performance	• What does the initiative plan provide to acknowledge success in implementation and reaching outcomes? • Are early wins defined and acknowledged? • What can we point to in terms of reward and recognition?
Environment	Comprised of Tools, Expectations, and Time	
Tools	Ready access to the tools and resources required for successful performance	• What tools does the initiative currently provide to support successful performance? • What evidence do we have that these tools are working as intended? • Are there tools or resources that performance requires that are (a) missing or (b) incomplete?
Expectations	Clear expectations, sometimes through policy, that align with successful performance	• Does current policy align with any and all related initiative elements? • Are expectations for performance made clear to those responsible for implementation? For outcomes? • Are clearly articulated expectations shared with, and incentivized for, performers?
Time	Time required to perform is made available	• Is the necessary time for implementation allocated? • Are other competing assignments considered and addressed, so that necessary time is made available?

Here's some hypothetical findings of a triage, based on the human performance drivers and the realm of possibilities in play with our case studies. I've noted the probable cause or causes for each.

NETS	Fifth-Grade Camp
Spotty implementation has plagued the program since its start.	Teachers have asked, "Why must I keep doing this?" and "Couldn't the paid camp teacher-counselors handle it?"
Possible findings: a. The program's implementation hasn't been evaluated; it's unclear what is and isn't happening. Those leading the program have no clear measure of fidelity or of the barriers that are getting in the way of full implementation (knowledge or skill, incentives in the form of feedback on performance). b. Some principals of teachers in the program lack an understanding of their role (knowledge or skill). Others fail to contribute in the ways they have been defined (assuming role is defined, the barrier is likely incentives, motivation-value, and/or motivation-confidence—you'd want to know more). c. New elementary teachers aren't accessing the online resources provided because some don't know they exist (knowledge or skill), while others find the website impossible to navigate (environment), and still others see no point in their use (motivation-value).	Possible findings: a. Roles for visiting teachers haven't been identified (environment). Rather, they're simply left to "do as they wish" during the five-day program. b. Expectations have been loosely defined, but teachers remain unsure and worry they're not doing the "right" thing, so they simply give up (motivation-confidence). c. When they participate, the camp teacher-counselors don't seem to notice; when they don't participate, it's the same (incentives, which, in turn, lower motivation-value). d. Teachers suggest they're unclear on what exactly to do and how their contributions complement the teacher-counselors, while making for a better experience for their students (knowledge or skill, and probably environment too).

Risks of foregoing the human performance triage I describe above:

- As educators, we often assume when something isn't happening, training will fix it.
- In either of these crises, you could assume it's a knowledge or skills problem, jump in and train them.
- If you did that for NETS, you'd not fully solve any of the hypothetical findings.
- If you did that for Fifth-Grade Camp, you'd not solve a, b, or c, and likely only partially solved.

A few more words about human performance technology are merited.

It doesn't matter what crisis your initiative is facing. Sometimes the crisis will involve participants not achieving the defined outcomes—meaning, they are unable to perform as described by the initiative outcomes. When this happens, triage using the questions above, as relevant, to get yourself into the shoes of participants and understand how they experience each category.

- If your initiative targets student performance and student-focused outcomes, I'd want to hear from students. And yes, I'd ask the questions using age-appropriate and relevant phrasing, based on the students and your initiative's focus.

- If your initiative involves outcomes for teachers or leaders, I'd again pursue answers to relevant questions, based on the outcomes involved.

The magic of the **human performance barrier/driver categories** extends beyond the participants your initiative targets. You can also use them to triage crises related to implementation or really anything else.

- If your team hasn't been able to implement accordingly to plan, use the questions to explore and understand the barriers that are getting in their way.

- If higher-ups aren't supporting your initiative like you intended, use the questions and categories to consider whether the barrier is lack of knowledge, motivation specific to valuing the effort, or even access to the right tools (think evidence and data) to understand the import and impact.

Defaulting to the Familiar: Beware the Skills/Knowledge Driver

As you saw in the hypothetical findings, defaulting to the familiar training or professional development may not solve the crisis you face. Know that roughly 80% of the time, when something isn't happening, it is caused by something *other than* lack of skills or knowledge or in addition to a lack of skills or knowledge (Stolovitch & Maurice, 1998). Said another way, 80% of the time when what we want to have happen doesn't, only 20% of the time is it solely caused by a lack of skills or knowledge. So, keep your eyes open for the barriers at play as you work to address your initiative crises. Addressing one crisis, when perhaps two or three are in play, means missed opportunities and a less than fully improved situation.

15. Fidelity Check-up

I regularly encounter educators who share their bad relationships with the concept of fidelity. During the accountability movement, some teachers were required to deliver instruction in narrowly defined, specifically orchestrated ways. The specifications and requirements, which were contained in everything from lesson plans and textbooks to actual "teaching scripts," were typically enforced through the call for fidelity of implementation. When you deviated from the specification, you were not implementing with fidelity. Teacher and leader alike developed a negative opinion of fidelity because, at times, they were forced to deny their own professional expertise in favor of the press for compulsory fidelity.

Yet, there is an effective space that combines fidelity with the application of professional expertise. It is one where our initiatives benefit from specific guidelines for their implementation, while providing latitude for experienced implementers who tailor the initiative for the unique needs of their participants. The challenge for leaders designing initiatives is to describe and require fidelity in areas that are central to the initiative, while creating space for customization outside those non-negotiable and defining imitative elements.

Use this checklist to assess and document each fidelity dimension of your initiative in the current crisis setting. Then, where needed, take action using the guidance at the checklist's end.

Before you review the checklist, here are some related elements that are important to understand.

Component	Description
Defined	Has the dimension been defined for the initiative in overt, measurable ways?
Shared Expectation	Is there shared understanding of the expectation among those implementing the initiative? In other words, is everyone on the same page about what's to happen?
Latitude	There should be room to implement with fidelity while also providing latitude to tailor the implementation to unique needs as determined by the expertise of those doing the implementation. In the absence of that latitude, they may simply give up.

	Fidelity Dimensions	Defined?	Shared Expectation?	Latitude?
1	Expectations—specific to the content, frequency, duration, and coverage of the initiative's implementation			
2	Exposure/Dose—of initiative in which participants are required to engage to benefit (establish dosage boundaries to define successful participation)			
3	Quality of Implementation—of initiative implementation (e.g., quality of leadership, program oversight, coaching, teaching, etc.)			
4	Reactions of People Involved—how we intend to ensure our teachers and students—or whomever the initiative engages—find relevance in their participation			
5	Initiative Differentiation—how we intend to make certain our initiative is unique and different from others that may address similar outcomes			

Taking Action

Defined:
- For fidelity dimensions that are undefined, work with your team to reach clarity and document your expectations.
- Note: Make sure those expectations are shared and agreed to as well.

Shared Experience:
- Share the defined list of fidelity expectations with those responsible for implementing the initiative.
- Engage in dialogue about the expectations and hear any concerns from those engaged in implementation.
- Consider adjustments based on concerns, as necessary.
- Reach agreement across the team about each fidelity dimension.

Latitude:
- Discuss each fidelity dimension with the team specific to where it sits on a "one size fits all" versus a "professional judgment" implementation expectation.
- Work toward agreement on each dimension as to the amount of latitude that will be acceptable to the team.
- Document this "professional judgement" element for each fidelity dimension.

Using our NETS case study, here are some hypothetical actions the team could take to further define fidelity for their program, which might be pursued through this exercise. Note that there would be additional fidelity definitions reviewed and defined for each implemented component of the initiative.

	Fidelity Dimensions	Next Steps: Moving Toward Defined
1	Expectations—specific to the content, frequency, duration, and coverage of the initiative's implementation	• Review currently defined expectations for level of detail. • Quantify, or further quantify as necessary, how often NETS will convene teachers from across the district, the prioritized content of the initiative (based on needs—see below), and the expectations for site-level (principal) involvement.
2	Exposure/Dose—of initiative in which participants are required to engage to benefit (establish dosage boundaries to define successful participation)	• Define minimum levels of participation for new teachers and their site leaders. • Implement a "contract" or other agreement document to seal participation of both new teachers and, in their supporting role, site leaders.
3	Quality of Implementation—of initiative implementation (e.g., quality of leadership, program oversight, coaching, teaching, etc.)	• Review expectations of both initiative leaders and site leader contributions specific to success criteria (program quality). Define and refine as necessary. • Conduct formative program evaluation to determine quality of implementation, including quality-focused feedback on initiative leadership and support provided, as defined, at the site level.
4	Reactions of People Involved—how we intend to ensure our teachers and students—or whomever the initiative engages—find relevance in their participation	• Add formative program evaluation to check in with new teachers quarterly—including assessing new, partially, and fully met needs. • Collect principal perspective on observed program impact and, in particular, the program's success in meeting retention goals. • Revise program mid- and end-of-year in a continuous improvement cycle toward meeting teacher and school needs.
5	Initiative Differentiation—how we intend to make certain our initiative is unique and different from others that may address similar outcomes	• Review initiative design to ensure it reflects both national research on new elementary teacher needs and the district's priorities and unique needs. • Define or refine initiative, where necessary, to fully reflect local needs and priorities while leveraging best practice in supporting the new elementary teacher experience.

16. Backing Your Way Into the Perfect Solution

My colleague Peggy O'Brien has contributed her amassed talents to diverse organizations, from the District of Columbia Public Schools as assistant superintendent, to becoming vice president of the Corporation for Public Broadcasting's Education Unit, and of late, director of education for the Folger Shakespeare Library. Our many collaborations have measurably shaped my understanding of initiatives.

One piece of learning relates to fixing programs in crisis and that point where you're considering a range of solutions such as new program components, alternate investments, enhanced human resources, compensation elements, and the list goes on. Early and inevitably in these conversations someone at the table brings up money. I've watched many sweetly flowing, solution-oriented brainstorming sessions turn immediately and intolerably sour as the result of a too-early interjection of fiscal concerns. When we're ideating solutions for crisis, it's going well, and then budget-related cold water douses that process, what's a leader to do?

I've witnessed this approach working flawlessly. In the situations I've described, the leader simply acknowledges there's a time for consideration of budget, and that time is 100% *not now*. She leads her team to set the concern aside and to continue to surface what, in an ideal world, would be the perfect solutions. Here's what typically happens as a result:

- People become unfettered from the proverbial chains tying them to a budget that may, or may not, be immovable—a determination that cannot possibly be made until the full set of ideal solutions comes into focus.

- People begin to expand their thinking as ideas flow. Often, the creativity of the proposed solutions advances in this perfect space where hard monetary realities have been suspended, for now.

- As the final **solution set** forms, you observe it to be quite elegant in terms of its components, the actions you will take, and, most importantly, how those elements fit together in meaningful ways. You've created a system of solutions to affect predictable improvement to your crisis and initiative. As another mentor of mine, Allison Rossett, used to say, "You'll not be throwing Jello at the wall and praying it sticks."

Did I forget something? Oh yes ... the money. Eventually, it must come into the discussion. What I've learned by watching Peggy is what I'd describe as a sort of *reverse successive approximation* exercise to back into the perfect, executable solution. Take the output of your ideal solution ideation and step through the following checklist.

Here's a three-step process to refresh your thinking and move to the "right" solution, which, for me, is the **ideal** solution after we've adjusted for constraints and limitations that make reaching ideal not possible. Outcomes frame this entire process.

	Step	Your Approximation Steps Toward the "Right" Solution
1	Assign a price tag— this is the **real price** that will fully get it done.	Start by assigning a price tag to the full solution you've crafted. • Make it realistic, but don't feel the need to pad the number beyond that. • Ask yourself, what amount of money would be necessary to make this happen successfully and as we have defined it? • Consider human resource costs, the timeline on which the program will operate, as well as materials and logistics–like meeting space and food if those are relevant to your people and program.
2	Take that number and make the call: **Can it happen?**	You have the ideal solution. And you have determined the financial resources you need to make it happen. ❑ Can you picture a world where those funds are available? ❑ What other funding do you have at arm's length that might be transitioned to support your program in crisis? ❑ As you contemplate building up this faltering program, are there other programs that should be analyzed for deimplementation, thus freeing resources?
3	If the answer is **No**, you'll next take a minor step away from the perfection solution, but it is still in full sight.	If the perfect solution cannot receive the resources necessary for a true and fidelitous implementation toward the outcomes you've defined for those participating, it's time to scale back. • Do this in "baby steps," by walking away from that perfect solution you've framed. • As you do, what is the element you first lose sight of? Is it gone, or is it really just reduced in size? And what implications does that have for the available funding? • Still not there? Take another small step back and repeat the process just described. You'll be carefully weighing the relative importance of each component and the degree to which it needs to be fully present in your initiative.

The process I've describe is what I call reverse successive approximation. Applied to initiatives in crisis, we're using the process in reverse by starting with that perfect outcome as our center and peeling off the layers we cannot afford or fully afford, and the layers we may not need. We're also looking around us for swamped boats (see Strategy 20)—because if we advance a critical initiative through resources gained from an initiative that may already need adjustment, the time may be right to make that call too.

17. "Early" Wins

Jody Spiro, former director of education leadership at the Wallace Foundation, suggests that **early wins** come from early successes that point to change happening (Spiro, 2012). Since initiatives always involve some sort of change, defining early wins is most certainly relevant.

Initiative leaders should define early wins as part of their initiative plan, and there are multiple ways to do this. For example.

- Define implementation milestones and celebrate the early accomplishments when those milestones are met.

- Achieve shorter-term outcomes that are typically described in an initiative plan or logic model.

Regardless of the "what" behind the early wins, the point is to define them, pursue them, and then celebrate their achievement. In doing so, we

- intentionally draw attention to the initiative and the accomplishments, and then

- sustain that attention from one win to the next.

When your initiative is in crisis, early wins may be the last thought on your mind. But it is a relevant and important tool when it comes to making initiatives successful and recovering from a faltering state. While powerful on their own, early wins can be like icing on the cake because they naturally complement any other crisis resolution solutions you pursue. Think about achieving these outcomes with the early wins you'll define.

- Building in early wins is a natural and complementary way to gain and hold the attention of everyone even remotely involved.

- By defining, pursuing, and celebrating each early win, you can gain and sustain the attention of all the people who matter, embracing those who are implementing the initiative and those who must support it.

- People involved in the day-to-day implementation almost always "feel" the crisis when an initiative faces challenges.

- Recovering from crisis, no matter the type or types faced, is a team effort, and early wins can unite a team in a shared direction.

As you think about early wins for your program, don't forget their definition: Early wins are "successes demonstrating concretely that achieving the change goals is feasible and will result in benefits for those involved" (Spiro, 2012, p. 10).

	Early Wins Area	Early Wins Examples
1	Fidelity	• Celebrate steps to define or refine fidelity as an initial step on the road out of crisis. • Celebrate coming to agreement around shared expectations about fidelity from all responsible for implementing the program.
2	Road out of Crisis	• Celebrate reaching consensus on your revised initiative plan/approach (to come out of crisis).
3	Implementation	Coin some early wins around reaching the earliest steps toward fidelitous implementation. For example: • Initial training completed for all participants • Everyone incorporating the new program into their first lesson plan • Everyone teaching their first lesson • All students having received a laptop • 100% attendance at the first PLC • Everyone bringing a piece of data to share at the first PLC • All school principals posting their welcome message to their school's website
4	Promising Results	• Celebrate each student's initial mastery of the first new math lesson content. • Share teacher progress in implementing the new curriculum to formally demonstrate the early change that is happening. • Document early changes in participant perspectives that align with your initiative goals and outcomes (typically documented through program evaluation).
Some additional early win examples that make use of our case study scenarios		
	NETS Example	• Each new elementary teacher receives recognition for completing their first, second, and third month in the classroom. • Each site leader–new teacher pair is acknowledged and given reinforcing feedback upon submitting their first-year support plan using the initiative planning tools. The entire group is acknowledged and celebrated when submissions are complete for the entire district.
	Fifth-Grade Camp Example	• The initiative's leadership team celebrates completion of new criteria to guide classroom teacher participation while at camp. • At the end of Day 2, for each week's participants, classroom teachers are recognized by camp teacher-counselors for their participation and contributions to the camp experience.

Here are two more, admittedly unusual, early wins I've coined for initiatives in crisis:

1. Celebrating each elementary teacher's first failure integrating engineering content into their STEM curriculum. This came from the adoption of the Next Generation Science Standards and the simple fact that engineering is challenging and has typically gone unaddressed in many elementary school programs.

2. Celebrating an early increase in the reporting of bullying incidents on campus. This resulted from a program designed to reduce bullying through education. We celebrated this "early win" as an indicator of raised awareness and, hopefully, trust in the new systems put into place.

The point is, you can be incredibly creative in the definition of early wins. Just remember to think about logical accomplishments that are both measurable and hold value in terms of motivating your initiative's participants.

18. Navigating the White Space

My colleagues Sarah Milo Hoskow and Rachel Strang head up the Partner Experience and Implementation efforts of inquirED, a resource for K–5 social studies curriculum. They offered the following observation about their work and one of the challenges in supporting leaders and schools in their implementation of social studies curricula.

We see so many district leaders do thoughtful planning, develop an elaborate vision, etc. But all their stakeholders are not aware! For example, when we talk about vision for social studies instruction, leaders often say, "I've got the vision," but we are sometimes left wondering if the vision has been communicated *and* understood by teachers and other stakeholders.... Before we can even check for buy-in there needs to be understanding.

Other strategies have addressed public relations planning and strategic messaging. But those strategies work only when they reach the right people. Navigating the white space is an important concept on the road to crisis recovery and crisis avoidance too.

What is "white space?" Picture the organizational structure of your district or school. Likely there is an organization chart that sets forth who is responsible for what and who reports to whom. Based purely on this structure, it should be easy to know who to go to at any given time. If only it were that simple. This is where "white space" comes into play because most of the "getting things done" happens between the boxes on that organization chart.

You likely have spent much time and energy developing a vision and plan for your initiative. No doubt, your understanding of what's happening is deep. But can you say the same for those around you? And, as you've begun implementing, has your initiative fallen prey to the unexpected influence of the white space?

Here's a checklist to help you identify where and what is happening, while also leveraging the white space to support your crisis resolution efforts.

Use this checklist to surface white space elements that may be influencing your initiative. Then, craft a plan for how you will address each element you raise.

	Description	Your Findings and Plans
1	Does your initiative plan reflect the "real" way things are done in your organization, or is it dependent on how they "should" be done?	
2	Are there unwritten relationships in the white space of your organization that are challenging your initiative?	
3	Who was left out of the plan who now is a known and necessary ally?	
4	Are you intentionally bringing together the varied and diverse people and teams across your organization to support your initiative, even those who are tangentially, yet necessarily, involved?	
5	Thinking beyond the boxes, are there other people or teams—even those who at face value seem only remotely related—that could support your way out of crisis?	

You've probably observed effective leaders, especially those in huge districts, who seem to effortlessly dance through and around the white space in their organizations. Admittedly that is due, at least in part, to the relationships they have built over time. But it is also attributable to their dedication to legitimizing their work and responsibilities by doing the following:

- Continuously scanning the horizon for even small connections that facilitate their work
- Seeing the landscape for the system that it is and leveraging it to facilitate their work
- Thinking out of the box to anticipate and access the support of people and resources across the organization—long before they need it
- Leveraging the first three strategies to inform and motivate folks across the organization as they build momentum for their work, raise the initiative's profile, and ensure its success

These are far from impossible tasks. They take time and must be done with intention. But they also involve skills and strategies successful leaders already possess. Applying them to the white space will not only help your initiative recover from crisis but also pave the way for future initiatives you may just find yourself leading.

Sustaining and Scaling Crises

There are two additional types of crises that affect programs once they are well established. These are crises that result from success. In fact, I've heard people reference them as the punishment for succeeding! One is the struggle to keep the program alive; the other is the struggle to take the program to new and novel contexts. Here's how you'll know them when you see them.

Recognizing a Sustaining Crisis

You've implemented your program to plan. Perhaps you've even faced and triumphed over some crises along the way. The upshot is you've felt the satisfaction that comes from leading a successful, results-producing effort. It may have taken a year to achieve, or it may have

Everyone's saying, "Do more with less." But I can't run a program with less.

Those five years flew by. With no more grant funding, how are we going to keep this initiative afloat?

I was assuming bigger is better, but maybe we need to take a hard look at what is, and isn't, necessary for success in new settings.

We expanded the program to five new schools, but when I visit them, it certainly looks nothing like the program we started here.

I thought we could just expand this program and we'd see almost the same results... but that's not what's happening

taken five years. The point is, the program is in place, it's fully implemented, and the skies around it are blue. This is typically the time when thoughts turn to other programs: new or additional initiatives that may or may not complement your "first born." I've watched many leaders be seduced away from their high-performing initiatives simply because of their success. And many go willingly, to rightly pursue new challenges and areas of impact. But just because the program is running at "cruise altitude" and things appear to be on autopilot doesn't mean the program will run by itself—without human and physical resources, oversight, and dedicated continuous improvement efforts.

Another sustaining crisis scenario comes at the end of a funded program. With the support of grant or contract monies, you've successfully designed and implemented a high-performing program. But now, say it has been five years and the funding concludes, how do you sustain that meaningful program as the financial resources dwindle?

Let's boil the triggers of sustaining crises down to a finite set:

1. Originally funded by a grant or gift, the program reaches the end of the funding period.

2. The program leader's talent generates much success, but the leader now moves on to a new assignment.

3. The program leader's talent generates so much success that it's decided the leader will now manage an additional program (or five additional programs—yes, I've watched it happen more than once).

4. The program success causes people to believe "it's running itself," and all attention turns elsewhere. Those who are left implementing the program feel the vacuum the higher-ups don't see.

5. Budgets go through their typical cycles, and the successful program is challenged to "do more with less."

That last one is a doozy when it comes to understanding the logic. In lean times, you might be surprised how our funding victims are disproportionally the *successful* programs. The rationale heard is that given reduced funding, we should reallocate to our greatest areas of need. Yet, many a successful program has withered from the false belief that successful programs reach a point of needing little to no resources and oversight.

Recognizing a Scaling Crisis

Unlike the sustaining crisis, which requires action to simply keep a good thing going, the scaling crisis can appear when you're trying to take that good thing and expand it. Yes, successful initiatives can be magnetic. When we find something that works, something that yields predicable results for our students, teachers, or leaders, we want others to benefit. This involves bringing an established program to a wider group of participants, often in new and novel contexts. But what happens when your efforts to scale that successful program end up producing new, scaled implementations that fail to produce the great results you achieved with the initial program?

Surprisingly, there isn't as much written about scaling educational initiatives and programs as one might think. Here are the ones I encounter with frequency:

• Assumptions that what worked to achieve success in school or district X will automatically work in school or district Y.

- Not taking the time to carefully consider the success factors of the program intended for scaling to determine the key program elements that are critical to the program's success and estimate how much they could be modified (or stretched) by, and within, the new context.

- Lack of any dedicated needs assessment for the new and novel setting(s) into which the program will be scaled—to understand the extent to which the audience, needs, and environment match the original setting in which the program was successful.

- The "This program runs itself" fallacy, which is the false assumption you can "transplant" a successful program without similar, sometimes even greater, resources relative to the original implementation. Sure, economies of scale can be realized, but my experience in these situations is that people overestimate the economies they can expect.

- A failure to refine the program for each new setting. Studies suggest the need to refine programs for context, again requiring flexibility. Otherwise, as Elmore (1996) suggests, they'll become "caricatures" of their original design as they increasingly become a square peg being jammed into a round hole.

Strategies to Address Sustaining and Scaling Crises

The pages that follow provide a handful of tools that have positively affected both sustaining and scaling crises faced by my own initiatives or, more often, those I've been retained to evaluate. Admittedly these days, I'm more often called in to "fix" programs, and the tools have proved just as helpful in those situations too.

Here are the sustaining and scaling tools that will support your way out of these crises.

- Finding Your 80/20: Defining the core work of your initiative to focus your efforts on the actions that drive impact

- Don't Swamp the Boat: A collaborative exercise in reviewing individual initiatives as well as the ecosystem of programs being offered and identifying those weighing you down and those lifting you up

- Subtracting After You've Added—Deimplementation: Planning for the deimplementation of unnecessary or ineffective initiative components

- Phasing Implementation Over Time—Chunking Your Way Out of Crisis: Focusing your initiative's implementation by prioritizing and sequencing its elements over time

- Academic Return on Investment (A-ROI): Calculating the "bang for your buck," in terms of growth versus initiative investment, or comparing possible solutions based on their projected A-ROI

19. Finding Your 80/20

You've probably heard of the 80/20 rule (Juran, 1974). Often referenced as the Pareto principle, Juran's 80/20 rule comes from the business literature and, later, the total quality movement. The concept is pretty simple: About 20% of the causes produce around 80% of the results. Take a moment to think that through as applied to programs and initiatives: As leaders, of the total effort (call it 100%) we give to a program, it's really just one-fifth (call it 20%) of our efforts that produce most (four-fifths, or 80%) of the total results.

Pareto is a helpful heuristic to keep in mind when we are contemplating the scaling of programs. I want to be very careful *not* to promote the kinds of misuse this principle has seen over the years: This is *all conceptual and far from an exact science;* 80/20 provides helpful observations rather than absolute direction. Used proactively, the same actions support planning for scaling. What's more, it is also helpful when facing a sustaining crisis—especially if you're faced with the challenge to do more with less. The approach can identify where you'll make your investments when resources become scarce.

Let's apply the Pareto principle to a sustaining or scaling crisis (or opportunity).

Follow these three steps to conduct your own 80/20 exercise.

	Step	What You'll Do

1	Getting Started	• If you have a logic model, this is the perfect time to use it.
		• If you do not have a logic model,
		  – Proceed to the logic model tool and build out one to represent your initiative.
		  – Then, pursue this 80/20 exercise.
		  – Alternatively, in the absence of a logic model and for purposes of an 80/20 exercise, you could simply create a list of (1) all the different initiative components, and (2) the tasks or actions each component involves to fully implement.

2	Jumping In	• First, gather your team and review the allocation of initiative implementation investments in terms of time dedicated.
		  – Using some version of the following worksheet, assign each program component and its corresponding activities a percentage.
		  – The result should indicate, of the total time invested in the program (100%), what percentage is being dedicated to each component.
		  – This initial step will help you become aware of how time is currently being spent.
		
		• Next, apply the 80/20 rule.
		  – Returning to the 80/20 worksheet, use the next set of columns to review and estimate the influence of each initiative component on the total impact achieved. I call this assigning an *influence factor*.
		  – Press yourself to make these decisions based on all evidence you have. If you lack evidence, I strongly suggest you review the data crisis chapter and pursue at least a bit of extant data that you can use to inform your 80/20 effort.
		  – In this step you uncover the priority initiative components that are contributing to the majority of your results.

3	Reflect, Plan, and Prioritize	• Returning to the worksheet, review the initiative components and tasks you've listed. I suggest you sort them in descending order, with the greatest influencers leading your list.
		• Review and come to agreement about the list you're created.
		• Now, challenge the team with the following questions:
		  – Do our investments of time and resources match and each component match the influence factor we've assigned?
		  – How can we reallocate our time and resource investments such that they are focused on the components with the greatest influence factor(s)?
		  – Are there components on the list with low influence factors that we can eliminate from the initiative? When forced to make difficult choices, which components can be reduced or removed with the least or no impact on the initiative's impact?

Program Component and Related Tasks *These should be the processes/outputs from your logic model. If defined at a very high level, you may need to break them down further into tasks.*	Percentage of Total Time Allocated	Influence Factor: *Percentage of the total initiative results attributable to each component (or task)*	Reprioritized Time for Future Allocation
Component 1:			
Task 1:			
Task 2:			
Task 3:			
Task 4:			
Component 2:			
Task 1:			
Task 2:			
Task 3:			
Task 4:			
Component 3:			
Task 1:			
Task 2:			
Task 3:			
Task 4:			
Totals	**100%**	**100%**	**100%**

The benefits of the 80/20 exercise lie equally in the process and the results. It forces you to consider what is, and isn't, contributing to the results you're seeing. The dialog in which you'll engage will also surface new understandings that describe strengths and weaknesses of the initiative which you can pursue in your course correction effort.

The following table uses the NETS case study processes as an example.

Program Component and Related Tasks	Percentage of Total Time Allocated	Influence Factor: *Percentage of the total initiative results attributable to each component*	Reprioritized Time for Future Allocation
Training: Three times a year professional development targeting (1) pedagogy, (2) classroom management, and (3) collective efficacy	25%	20%	25%
Professional Learning Communities (PLCs): Site-based PLCs, overseen by site leaders and specifically positioned to engage, excite, and encourage teachers new to the school	10%	Unsure	0%
Resources: New teacher just-in-time supports around teaching and classroom management; frequent tips in a biweekly newsletter to new teacher-participants	45%	25%	25%
Peer Relationships: Fostering of connections and relationships between new teachers, establishing them as co-conspirators and co-supporters, as they cope with their entry into the profession	5%	25%	20%
Coaching Relationship: Ongoing one-on-one mentoring from site leader, coordinated with other program elements, to effectively "catch" teachers at crisis points and provide a safety net for remaining in the profession.	15%	30% (when it happens)	30%
Totals	**100%**	**100%**	**100%**

Consider the following, hypothetical findings from the NETS team's 80/20 exercise.

- The team considered and came to consensus on each program component—the time they were investing and its proportion of the total initiative positive outcomes.
- They realized, as a result of the scoring and dialogue that ensued, that PLCs, while a helpful experience, were not well integrated or aligned with the outcomes they wanted to effect. They decided to reinvest that effort elsewhere.
- They also noted that when the new teachers were regularly coached by their site leader, it was observed to have a tremendous impact on the new teacher's persistence. As a result, they doubled their future implementation investment here, including spending more time supporting site leaders who were not yet realizing fidelity in the implementation of their coaching.
- All agreed resources were important and helpful, when used. But all also agreed they could be further honed and produced less frequently (or adopted from existing materials), resulting in reallocation of part of the investment.

20. Don't Swamp the Boat

My amazing colleague Nancy Frey has become fond of the phrase "swamping the boat." A swamped boat may be the deimplementation you didn't know you needed. Let's use the swamped boat analogy and find parallels between schools and schooners. First, some boat background to frame our inquiry.

- Overloading a boat slows it down by reducing the portion of the vessel that is above water.

- Reducing the portion above the water level encourages the taking on of water, further weighing things down and slowing the movement.

- A weighed-down boat is unstable and, typically, unbalanced.

- Instability makes it more susceptible to outside forces, like heavy and rogue waves.

- Outside forces acting on an unstable vessel can quickly capsize it, leaving behind the vessel and everything it was trying to carry.

- The swamped boat is even at risk going to anchor, as lowering the anchor from the bow can quickly send unstable weight forward and tip things over.

Programitis, as I've termed it, is like a swamped boat. Too many programs weigh a school and district down, while making it more susceptible to the threats and challenges that are inevitable with time. Conversely, making your boat lean in right and intentional ways ensures efficient, forward sailing. It also makes it possible to anchor when the time is right without fear of tipping things over and losing everything on board.

Because this analogy has so many dimensions, I find it effective when exploring the complement of initiatives in a school or the range of initiatives across a district. The goals of this exercise are multiple and include the following:

- Taking inventory of everything that is running—whatever state it's in—and the resources (weight) each requires

- Assessing the weight and balance of your boat, once you have those programs and initiatives aboard

- Pursuing what I call sea trials, where you simulate possible disasters—from the mild to the wild—and talk through how you'd recover

At the conclusion of the exercise, you'll walk away with new insights about the programs that surround you every day. You'll have predicted risk and, as a result, be in a much better place to address it when something inevitable *tips the boat,* or your challenged to *add new cargo* in an already laden vessel.

With your team, use this exercise to explore program or initiative allocations, along with risks to their successful implementation and impact. Getting the boat ready to sail, not to mention safely reach a destination, is a fine analogy for our initiative planning and crisis recovery. Make sure to review examples of typical findings on the following page.

Testing Seaworthiness

1	**Program Manifest:** ❑ Name the programs and initiatives going into the boat. ❑ Indicate their relative size and resource load in some way.
2	**Waterline:** Based on what you've found, draw where you think the waterline will stand in your boat full of initiatives.
3	**Assess Your Weight & Balance:** ❑ Will you float? ❑ How much water will displace? ❑ Where are you likely to take on water?
4	**Consider Your Prowess** ❑ Will your hull split the water with ease, as designed? ❑ Or is the water line too low for the hull to be efficient?

Talk Through These Sea Trials to Predict What Would Happen

❑ Run a simulation with your initiative boat where strong waves rocked it slowly, then much more aggressively, in the water. What did you predict would happen?

❑ Run a drill where shifting programs all slide to the back, lowering the stern. What would happen, how would you recover?

❑ Run a hypothetical in which your program boat is capsized. What are your immediate thoughts? If you could save only a few programs, what would they be... and why?

What might you find after reviewing your seaworthiness? Here are a few examples to illustrate the possibilities.

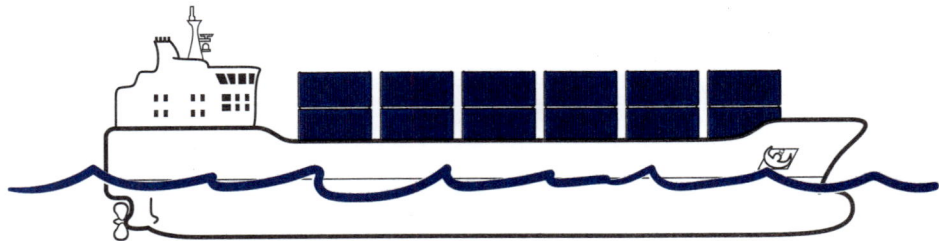

All of your initiatives, or all the components of a given initiative, are reasonable in scope and demand. Their presence, together, is easily accommodated and forward momentum is optimized given ideal placement at the waterline.

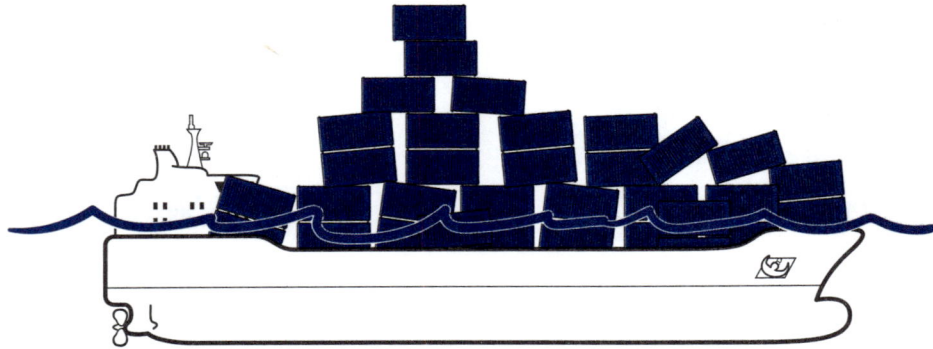

Too many initiatives, or too many components to a single initiative, weigh things down. Forward momentum is inefficient, laborious, or impossible given the high waterline of an overburdened vessel. Forward and rearview sightlines are blocked by the sheer number of initiatives or components with which you must contend. The weight and balance heightens risk of rough seas, or even being fully overturned. Prioritization and deimplementation should be considered.

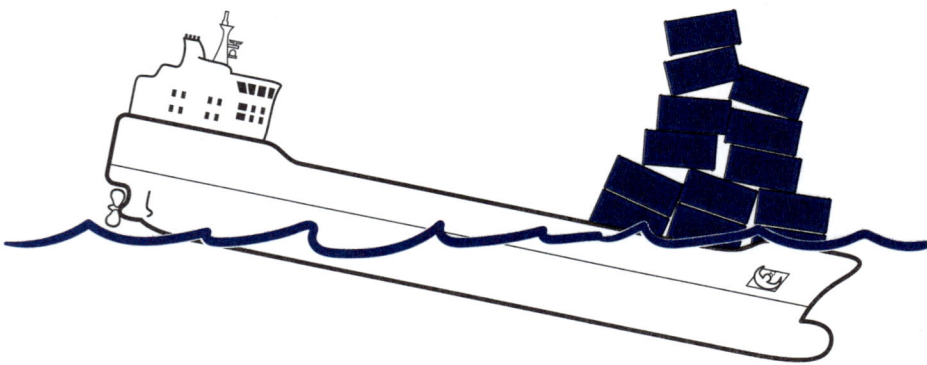

All of your initiatives, or all the components of a given initiative, are demanding attention at the same time. Resources are overallocated, with nothing getting implemented, let alone implemented well. The boat will capsize due because of imbalance and demand. Prioritization and deimplementation should be considered.

21. Subtracting After You've Added—Deimplementation

So much time, and so little to do, said no educator, ever.

The simple truth is, whether teacher, school leader, or district executive, it seems our plates are added to with increasingly regularity as each month goes by. New initiatives have a way of cropping up, whether driven by opportunity, need, or crisis. An overwhelmed teacher once said to me, in exhaustion, "I wish someone would tell me what *not* to do."

There is a response to that statement and it has a name: **deimplementation**. It's a strategy we've always needed and one that has finally begun receiving the attention it deserves. Deimplementation isn't so much about getting *rid of something*. Rather, it's *getting right about something*. Deimplementation challenges us to make informed, intentional decisions about the initiatives and programs into which we pour our time and talents, while sunsetting those programs and practices that are less likely to bear fruit.

When you realize, while implementing to scale or attempting to achieve a steady, sustained state, that you've not removed all the barriers necessary to make way for your initiative, you're likely facing a deimplementation crisis. Conflicting priorities, competing initiatives that take attention away from your program, or even existing policies and procedures that run counter to the very intent of your work, are examples of things that "get in the way" of a successful initiative. These are all examples of things that may need to be carefully "deimplemented" to make room for your initiative to thrive.

Deimplementation has roots in the medical field. There, the term describes "the process of reducing care that is harmful, ineffective, overused, or not cost-effective" (Wolf et al., 2021, p. 231). Education leaders, like DeWitt (2022), have observed the connection between these ideas and the work of educators. My efforts helping leaders explore a deimplementation opportunity suggests that these ideas are readily applicable to the education field.

When facing a program in crisis, including those resting in the scaling or sustaining phases, deimplementation can inform our planning and action.

	Deimplementation:			
	As Applied to Medicine (Wolf et al., 2021)	**As Applied to Education (Marshall, 2023)**	**As Applied to Your Initiative**	
			Questions	**Your Responses**
1	Developing benchmarks for low-value care for specific conditions so that doctors can be evaluated on their progress	Define benchmarks and evaluate the effectiveness of initiatives, programs, and strategies to differentiate low and high value	What evidence do we have that the program is providing value?	
			Relative to other programs, how is this one performing?	
2	Measuring the harms of overuse for children	Assess policies and practices that, when overused, result in negative outcomes for the program participants	What unintended or unexpected results is the program producing?	
			Are any of those results negative? If so, describe.	
3	Considering any potential unintended consequences of deimplementation.	Understand and protect successful elements of otherwise ineffective or low-value programs	What would be the result if this program was no longer present in our school or district?	
			Contemplate both the positive and negative results of deimplementation.	
4	Understanding the best ways to stop each type of low-value care	Carefully and intentionally plan the deimplementation process, typically for underperforming parts of a program, to bring about better states	What must we be mindful of when deimplementing any part of the program?	
			What steps should we follow in our deimplementation?	
			Consider timing, current participants, and the intersection with other programs.	

Here are some hypothetical responses that might result from the Fifth-Grade Camp team completing this exercise.

Deimplementation:		
As Applied to Education (Marshall, 2023)	**As Applied to Your Initiative**	
	Questions	**Your Responses**
1 Use defined benchmarks to evaluate the effectiveness of initiatives, programs, and strategies to differentiate low and high value.	What evidence do we have that the program is providing value?	• Most fifth graders say they enjoy the program. • Most parents appreciate the opportunity their children wouldn't otherwise have.
	Relative to other programs, how is this one performing?	• This program suffers from truly defined outcomes that can prove its worth. • While it is happening (i.e., students are going to camp), it is compulsory compared to other programs that are impact-driven. • Its true value has yet to be quantified. • Implementation, especially roles for the visiting classroom teacher, can be challenging. There has been significant pushback on teachers having to handle all logistics prior to the camp, while then having an ill-defined role during the camp, where their presence may not even matter.
2 Assess policies and practices that, when overused, result in negative outcomes for the program participants.	What unintended or unexpected results is the program producing?	• The program is resulting n cynicism among classroom teachers, specific to their participation, lack of involvement. • The program's impact has been hard to demonstrate, causing a troubling lack of hard evidence/results.
	Are any of those results negative? If so, describe.	• Roles for visiting teachers need to be more deeply conceptualized and documented. • Lack of clarity around outcomes is resulting in some negative perspect ve on the program.
3 Understand and protect successful elements of otherwise ineffective or low-value programs.	What would be the result if this program was no longer present in our school or district?	• Program is a long-standing tradition for fifth graders. • Removing it would take away a life experience that most urban students would never have.
	Contemplate both the positive and negative results of deimplementation.	• Deimplementing classroom teacher involvement could solve the immediate pushback and eliminate expectations around their support, which varies dramatically by teacher. • It would result in less supervision of students, less integration of the camp program with the classroom instruction, both before and following camp.

Deimplementation:			
As Applied to Education (Marshall, 2023)	**As Applied to Your Initiative**		
	Questions	**Your Responses**	
4	Carefully and intentionally plan the deimplementation process, typically for underperforming parts of a program, to bring about better states.	What must we be mindful of when deimplementing any part of the program?	• The deimplmentation must not result in more work or time allocation for classroom teachers. • If we chose to focus their role, we must find other ways to accomplish the logistical parts of their previous assignments.
		What steps should we follow in our deimplementation?	• First, plan for deimplementation of the teacher's logistical planning role. Optimize pre-camp planning and logistics centrally, while identifying central district supports that can relieve teachers of this considerable task.
		Consider timing, current participants, and the intersection with other programs.	• Second, redefine the teacher role from an instructional perspective. Create continuity among (a) preparing their students for the experience, (b) the teacher having an active teaching role during the camp itself, and (c) reinforcing the experience upon their return to the classroom.

22. Phasing Implementation Over Time—Chunking Your Way Out of Crisis

Who hasn't been fascinated by watching an expert plate spinner? While techniques vary, there is at least one non-negotiable in the art of plate spinning: You don't start 10 plates spinning all at once. Rather, you get one spinning, and spinning well, and then your turn your attention to one or two more, while not neglecting the first plate. The sense of accomplishment is realized when you have multitudes of plates spinning successfully and efficiently.

Scaling initiatives is a lot like spinning plates. Frankly, leading initiatives is too. While we may want to solve the world's problem in one fail swoop, we're ill advised to tackle things all at once. Make note: That holds true, no matter the program, the need, or the crisis. Why? Well, getting everything spinning all at once is near impossible, and the result can quickly crash to pieces in front of your eyes. Once that happens, gluing things back together to simply get another crack at it will be challenging, at best.

As a system thinker, I'm constantly ruminating on the different ways things can fit together, which necessarily means "trying on" a lot of possibilities that simply won't work, thus avoiding those rabbit holes. This thinking includes both groupings and sequences. Leading the implementation or expansion of a program requires both. But when you reach the crisis point, especially if you're scaling a program, it's time to wave the red flag, take a step back, and reflect on the pieces and processes.

Phasing implementation is a fancy way of phrasing a favorite term: chunking. Many of us are natural chunkers. When it comes to programs, chunking can be an especially useful strategy. Chunking a failing scaling effort into phases offers a way to reset and regain control and then move forward in a more measured and calculated way. Plus these "chunks" are also natural points for early wins on the road to recovery.

Note: if you're in crisis, you may actually choose to deimplement parts of your program for the time being. That's perfectly fine, and probably smart. In crisis, you may need to take a step back, in order to take a leap forward. If this exercise brings you to that conclusion, consider using the deimplementation strategy I've shared in the preceding tool to review your current program's individual elements and make decisions about what to set aside (deimplement) for now. In time, and with success, your plan can accommodate bringing them back. This is a fine example of the adage, "You've got to go slow to go fast."

Phasing Implementation Over Time Tool

This phasing tool will help you consider and organize your implementation tasks. It can be used when addressing any implementation crisis to plan a path that gets the initiative back on track. It is also highly useful when planning the scaling of an existing initiative. Let it guide your consideration of the full range of tasks, which are absolutely necessary, and the order in which each must occur.

Task	Dependencies	Triggers to Move Forward
Break down the various implementable parts of your program in stand-alone steps.	*List what is necessary to have in place to implement this task.*	*Describe the evidence you need to see that will trigger you to move forward with the next task.*
Think of each task as one "plate" in your series.	*What's necessary for this plate to spin?*	*What will constitute the plate spinning well enough to start a second plate spinning?*

Here is an excerpt of the results when the NETS team conducted this exercise specific to the following initiative component:

Resources: New teacher just-in-time supports around teaching and classroom management; frequent tips in a biweekly newsletter to new teacher-participants

Task	Dependencies	Triggers to Move Forward
Break down the various implementable parts of your program in stand-alone steps.	*List what is necessary to have in place to implement this task.*	*Describe the evidence you need to see that will trigger you to move forward with the next task.*
Think of each task as one "plate" in your series.	*What's necessary for this plate to spin?*	*What will constitute the plate spinning well enough to start a second plate spinning?*
Needs assessment, based on research into new elementary teacher needs and surveying our current teachers, to prioritize teaching and classroom management support tools	Dedicated team time to collect and prioritize support needs • Survey design and invitation • Survey responses • Summarized analysis results	The resulting prioritized list of teaching and classroom management supports will push us forward to the next task.
Design of first teaching or classroom management support tool, based on needs assessment priorities	Dedicated team time to ideate tool content and style • Review and produce tool content in draft form • Team review and tool optimization • Distribution to new teachers and site leaders	First tool is delivered to teachers and their site leader Three weeks' time for review and implementation is given
Rapid feedback from teachers and site leaders on initial tool	Dedicated time to solicit evaluative feedback for continuous improvement • Survey design and invitation • Responses rating tool content, relevance, results from use, strengths, and opportunities • Response that revisits needs to prioritize next tool's development	Summarized feedback to inform: • Revisions to direct optimization of first support tool • Priority content confirmed for focus of second support tool
Design of second teaching or classroom management support tool	(Process, including formative evaluation feedback loop and support tool optimization repeats.)	

While admittedly low-level, the process defined above reflects what is truly necessary to create an effective support tool that gets used by a given, specific group of people. Crisis appears when we just expect the right things to happen "automagically": "Can you whip up a support tool for teachers needing help with social contracts?" Being intentional means not only being realistic about what it will take to implement something, but also about making sure it is the "right" thing to implement, both before you implement it and afterward to understand and exact your impact.

23. Calculating Your Academic Return on Investment (A-ROI)

Ultimately, money must come into the picture. There is only so much of it, and educational leaders are charged with making the best, most informed decisions for allocating it in ways that make the most difference possible. Said another way, we want to heighten the return on investment, or ROI.

ROI has a long history in the business world. Many didn't see its place in education, specific to students and learning, since we're not looking to make a profit. Yet, every program should return something on the investment, even if that return isn't money. Enter a newer term, **academic return on investment (A-ROI)**, which is an equation for determining the return on investments using inputs of both student performance and budget expenditures (Frank & Hovey, 2014). The resulting A-ROI figure describes the assumed academic gain (hence, the "return") for each unit of cost (investment). Said another way, A-ROI answers the question, "How much academic outcome was achieved for our investment of $X into the program?"

The following tool is designed to help you perform your own A-ROI calculations for programs and initiatives that have the data they require. A quick observation: All well-designed initiatives should have these data. Going forward, my advice is to build them into the program or initiative plan, including making them part of the evaluation plan.

A warning is in order: While A-ROI is a helpful, educative figure to have for programs and initiatives, it is not sufficient in and of itself. Like most things in education, one number cannot tell the entire story. Therefore, think of A-ROI as a highly useful tool among the many tools in the needs assessment, program planning, and program evaluation toolsets. It's especially helpful when reviewing programs to compare their relative returns.

Academic Return on Investment offers an equation for calculating the "bang for your buck." It helps you understand what you're getting for your investment and even compare two different initiatives to understand their relative returns.

$$\text{Academic Return on Investment (A-ROI)} = \frac{\text{Learning Increase} \times \text{Number of Students Served}}{\text{Full Cost of Program or Initiative}}$$

The final result is typically multiplied by 100, due to learning increase being expressed as a percentage in the primary equation and, thus, the need for conversion.

	Data	What You'll Do
1	Learning Growth	• Gather your best measure of student growth resulting from the initiative. — Note that this can also work for calculating A-ROI for initiatives that target teachers or leaders. — You simply need to have some sort of pre-to-post, or growth over time, data for those the initiative engages. • The best measure is going to be that which is closest to the initiative content; avoid the more general or broad norm-referenced tests, unless they include discrete scores on a subtest that is well-matched to your initiative. • Make note that you need a growth figure for the initiative and, therefore, you likely need both a pre- and post-measure to reach the equation-required measure of growth.
2	Number of Students Served	• Next, determine the number of students who have been participants in the program or initiative. • Make sure to include only active participants in this count. This is because your A-ROI result should represent the true potential of the program when implemented as designed in your setting. That means including the people who experienced the program with fidelity. — Note: If attendance at a consistent level is part of your crisis, that likely requires an analysis other than A-ROI.
3	Reflect, Plan, and Prioritize	• Now, calculate the full cost of the program, which should necessarily include the program's cost, plus the following: — the teacher's salary (with benefits) for their time spent implementing the program — Cost for supporting resources or tools required by the program — Cost of space for the program to run, knowing that different programs require different spaces with different cost factors, and you may end up comparing the A-ROI on two programs with different space requirements and costs.
4	Calculate	• Finally, plug your numbers into the equation and calculate the A-ROI of your program or initiative. Remember to multiple the resulting figure by 100 if your growth in a percentage.

Here are some hypothetical examples of the A-ROI equation being applied to familiar initiatives.

Example 1: Tutoring Program

- Tutors enter all second-grade classrooms once a week to pull out the 10 students with the greatest need.
- Students were tested at the beginning of the year, and before Winter Break, using a math diagnostic, specific to the first semester content. The average growth for the 40 students was 30%.
- With four classrooms involved, the total number of students served is 40.
- The cost of the tutors for 40 students over the semester was $8,500.

A-ROI .14
Meaning, for each dollar spent, I can expect to see .14% average growth across the 40 students. $= \dfrac{30\% \text{ (expected growth)} \times 40 \text{ students}}{\$8,500 \text{ cost for evaluated period of time}}$

Note: The final figure is multiplied by 100 due to percentage figure in primary equation.

Thus, for every dollar invested in the tutoring program, we can expect an average .14% increment of growth, as measured by the math diagnostic used, across the population involved. You could run a parallel calculation for the remaining students who didn't receive tutoring and then compare results and opportunity costs.

Example 2: Phonics Program Decision

A-ROI is most helpful when comparing programs to inform decision making, including deimplementation decisions. Consider this example of two phonic programs. Even if the program is not in your district yet, you can likely run these scenarios if the program has done research and offers established growth figures. Of course, confirm that the growth figures you use come from schools or districts with characteristics and needs similar to your own.

Program Candidate 1: Phonics Fanatics

A-ROI = .90
Meaning, for each dollar spent, I can expect to see .9% average growth across the 500 students. $= \dfrac{45\% \text{ (expected growth)} \times 500 \text{ students}}{\$25,000 \text{ cost for evaluated period of time}}$

Program Candidate 2: Fun With Phonics

A-ROI = .66
Meaning, for each dollar spent, I can expect to see .66% average growth across the 500 students. $= \dfrac{20\% \text{ (expected growth)} \times 500 \text{ students}}{\$15,000 \text{ cost for evaluated period of time}}$

Current Phonics Program in School

A-ROI = .13
Meaning, for each dollar spent, I can expect to see .13% average growth across the 500 students. $= \dfrac{5\% \text{ (observed growth)} \times 500 \text{ students}}{\$20,000 \text{ cost for evaluated period of time}}$

Program Candidate 1 delivers a much higher A-ROI, relative to its competitor, when analyzed within this school's unique context. Of course, A-ROI doesn't make decisions for you. The difference in budget must also be considered in conjunction with the A-ROI figures and other factors. A-ROI does offer an elegant way to quantify and present costs and the resulting benefits, especially when comparing the value of different programs or initiatives.

A FINAL FIX

Evaluative Thinking

Together, we've focused on addressing the crisis or crises you're currently facing. Along the way, you've picked up any number of strategies and habits of mind, which you've found yourself beginning to apply across all dimensions of your leadership. Whether you're leading a district, school, or classroom; whether you're addressing a program or an initiative; and when you're assessing the performance of the people around you (teachers, staff, students), most of these strategies have wisdom to inform our thinking and doing.

Before things come to an end, there is one more frame of mind to offer. Think of it as a meta-strategy that is useful for both addressing and avoiding crisis. As someone who specializes in needs assessment and program evaluation, I have picked up and honed the habit of evaluative thinking along my own journey. But it is something successful leaders often do without even realizing it. Evaluative thinking provides a

- frame of mind through which I can see the world;

- set of ideas by which I come to understand what surrounds me;

- means by which to always challenge my own thinking and understanding;

- reminder to continually question, consider, and anticipate such that I identify and deflate looming challenges before they expand to full-blown crises (I call this appreciative crisis avoidance); and

- stronghold when I encounter messy situations, when my head begins to spin, and my nature is to become paralyzed not knowing where to start.

Evaluative thinking isn't magic. But it is something program evaluators do continuously and, when applied in appropriate ways and doses, it returns the benefits I've outlined. Schwandt and colleagues (2016), informed by Earl and Timperley (2015), described it this way:

> Evaluative thinking is a way of viewing the world, an ongoing process of critical reflection on, and appraisal of, assumptions and claims, coupled with a commitment to continuous learning and a willingness and ability to modify views in light of reasoned arguments and evidence. (p. 2)

24. Strategies for Evaluative Thinking

What follows are my principles of evaluative thinking. Far from original, they have been derived over the years from the influences of research and researchers, intuition, and more than 20 years of ground truth leading and evaluating programs.

Here are five key components of evaluative thinking. They're purposefully sandwiched between an overall call for evaluative thinking (Getting Critically Creative) and the ultimate reality-inducing question (The BIG Question), which nicely serve as anchors to evaluative thinking practice. As you learn these principles, you will find they can guide and inform your thinking about implementation and many other leadership endeavors.

	Evaluative Thinking Principle	Definition
	Getting Critically Creative	Patton (2018) has argued that evaluative thinking requires critical *and* creative thinking. For me, this is the overarching goal—to be both critical and creative about our initiatives: what's needed, how they're designed, how they're implemented, the results they produce, and the improvements they need. No matter what phase you're in, no matter what crisis you're facing, the elements below can guide your thinking and doing.
1	Make Informed Decisions—Then Do It Again and Again	Ideate and iterate. Based on what you objectively know, you'll make decisions, then make them again as you learn and your program marches forward.
2	Prioritize What's Provable With Evidence	Favor evidence of opinion. Find value in both quantitative and qualitative, credible data. Be mindful about who is determining whether something is, or isn't, credible such that you protect the full range of valid perspectives.
3	Pursue 360-Degree Viewpoints	Push yourself to understand the program from as many viewpoints as possible, including the viewpoints of participants, implementers, leaders, supporters, and funders. Where viewpoints might vary within a group, give voice to as many people as possible and practical.
4	Press to Understand Process and Outcome	Dedicate your evaluative thinking to both your program's process (implementation) and its outcomes (impacts), and explore the connections between the two. Remember that correlation doesn't necessarily equal causation, so identify, but be critical of, the observed connections between what you're doing (implementing) and what you're achieving (outcomes).
5	Conclude, Then Disprove	Memorialize the conclusions from your evaluative thinking alongside your interpretations regarding their "whys." Then, get creative by poking holes in those conclusions and challenging your own thinking.
	The BIG Question: What if it isn't the way I think it is?	Conclude an evaluative thinking cycle by asking what assumptions have been made in the process of understanding what's happening with our program. Remember that assumptions come into play both intentionally and unintentionally. Ask yourself: • Could I be fully misunderstanding what I see? • Would members of our different constituencies see this situation the way I do? • What are the consequences if our thinking is wrong?

Whether you're standing at a major initiative milestone, or simply taking time mid-implementation to reflect on progress, evaluative thinking offers a mind frame to understand your program, anticipate challenges, and continuously improve its performance.

A final thought on evaluative thinking may surprise you: It's *fun!* I find motivation in making things better, and I inform that process by challenging my own perspectives and assumptions. Consider this: Without evaluative thinking, we might still be thinking the world is flat. Critical and creative are two ideas that are typically viewed as mutually exclusive. Yet, this is a case where opposites attract to make the whole greater than the sum of its parts. Putting them together in an evaluative thinking exercise gives satisfaction, while leveraging both the left and right sides of the brain.

A Final Word

Evaluative thinking is the perfect strategy to conclude this crisis-combating guidance. It provides the perfect complement to any of the strategies you've employed. As you view your initiative landscape, take time to be critically creative by asking questions, seeking data, and challenging your own perspectives. But also take time to float new ideas, make longshot interpretations of what you see, engage in devil's advocating, and ask the "what ifs" that creatively expand your thinking. Admittedly, I'm always surprised how my own understanding, strategy, and ability to lead grow because of my evaluative thinking practice.

Glossary

Academic return on investment (A-ROI): the resulting A-ROI figure describes the assumed academic gain (hence, the "return") for each unit of cost (investment)

Appreciative inquiry: as applied to needs assessment, inquiry that seeks to understand strengths and possibilities; the opposite of and complement to deficit-based inquiry

Behavioral engineering: an approach to engineering success for a given set of participants (teachers, students) that provides them with the necessary skills/knowledge, motivation, incentives, and environmental supports

Deimplementation: the process of eliminating ineffective practices that, historically, have not produced results

Early wins: according to Spiro (2012), used to describe successes demonstrating concretely that achieving the change goals is feasible and will result in benefits for those involved

Evidence pockets: data, often unnoticed, underused, or underappreciated, that are already in existence and can be mined in support of your initiative's data needs

Extant data: documents, data, records, or other existing evidence that support your initiative's design, implementation, or impact

Fidelity: the extent to which the initiative's implementation matches the plan (e.g., the logic model processes and outputs)

Fresh eyes: setting aside your current understanding, presumptions, and biases and attempting to look at the situation anew

Gap analysis: the process of defining the difference between the current state and an ideal state

Get smart: an initial effort to understand the people and the need, the barriers and strengths at play, and what we will accept as successful outcomes

Ground truth: information that is known to be real or true; in our use, ground truth is information gained in the process of implementing a plan in the "real world" and describes the truths that come as a result

Human performance barrier/driver categories: barriers to performance and drivers of performance; the four categories are skills/knowledge, motivation value/confidence, incentives, and environment

Initiative: the initiative approach recognizes that careful attention to existing efforts and strengths, needs-driven design, leadership buy-in, connection to mission, priorities, and existing efforts are all necessary to produce and implement something that yields predictable results

Just-in-time data collection: a rapidly defined, highly foucsed, data collection effort, specific to a urgent data call, that is completed in a matter of hours or a few days

Logic model: a tool to represent an initiative's design consisting of, at a minimum, inputs, process/outputs, and outcomes

Programitis: an inflammation of programs within a school or district; too many programs such that at least some are not running as planned or with impact

Solution set: the sum total of all the different elements of your initiative that, when implemented together, will allow you to achieve predictable results

Theory of action: a series of if–then statements about the relationships between planned actions and expected results; describes how change will lead to results

References

Alexander, S. M. (2023). *A needs assessment: Mitigating the influence of adversity on college and career readiness by cultivating resilience and social capital in schools.* Publication No. 30813771. [Doctoral dissertation, San Diego State University]. ProQuest Dissertations and Theses Global. http://libproxy.sdsu.edu/login?url=https://www.proquest.com/dissertations-theses/needs-assessment-mitigating-influence-adversity/docview/2899497146/se-2

DeWitt, P. M. (2022). *De-implementation: Creating the space to focus on what works.* Corwin.

Doran, G. T. (1981). There's a SMART way to write management's goals and objectives. *Journal of Management Review, 70,* 35–36.

Earl, L., & Timperley, H. (2015). *Evaluative thinking for successful educational innovation.* OECD Education Working Papers, No. 122. OECD Publishing. https://doi.org/10.1787/5jrxtk1jtdwf-en

Elmore, R. F. (1996). Getting to scale with good educational practice. *Harvard Educational Review, 66*(1), 1–26.

Frank, S., & Hovey, D. (2014). *Return on investment in education: A "system-strategy" approach.* Education Resource Strategies (ERS). https://www.erstrategies.org/library/return_on_investment_in_education

Gilbert, T. F. (2007). *Human competence: Engineering worthy performance.* Pfeiffer.

Juran, J. M. (1974). *Quality control handbook* (3rd ed.). McGraw Hill.

Mager, R. F., & Pipe, P. (1997). *Analyzing performance problems: Or you really outta wanna* (3rd ed.). CEP Press.

Marshall, J. (2023). *Right from the start: The essential guide to implementing school initiatives.* Corwin.

Novak, J. D. (1998). *Learning, creating, and using knowledge: Concept maps as facilitative tools in schools and corporations.* Erlbaum.

Patton, M. Q. (2018). A historical perspective on the evolution of evaluative thinking. *New Directions for Evaluation, 158,* 11–28. https://doi.org/10.1002/ev.20325

Rossett, A. (2009). *First things fast: A handbook for performance analysis* (2nd ed.). Pfeiffer.

Rummler, G. A., & Brache, A. P. (1996). *Improving performance: Managing the white space in the organization chart.* Jossey-Bass.

Schwandt, T., Ofir, Z., D'Errico, S., & El-Saddik, K. (2016). Realising the SDGs by reflecting on the way(s) we reason, plan and act: The importance of evaluative thinking. https://doi.org/10.13140/RG.2.2.11995.59683

Spiro, J. (2012). Winning strategy: Set benchmarks of early success to build momentum for the long term. *Journal of Staff Development, 33*(2), 10–16.

Stolovitch, H. D., & Keeps, E. J. (Eds.). (1992). *Handbook of human performance technology.* Jossey-Bass.

Stolovitch, H. D., & Maurice, J. G. (1998). Calculating the return on investment in training: A critical analysis and a case study. *Performance Improvement, 37*(8), 9–20.

Utah Education Network. (2017). *UtahFutures Impact Evaluation.*

Wolf, E. R., Krist, A. H., & Schroeder, A. R. (2021). Deimplementation in pediatrics: Past, present, and future. *JAMA Pediatrics, 175*(3), 230–232.

Index

A Sage Company

CORWIN HAS ONE MISSION: to enhance education through intentional professional learning.

We build long-term relationships with our authors, educators, clients, and associations who partner with us to develop and continuously improve the best evidence-based practices that establish and support lifelong learning.

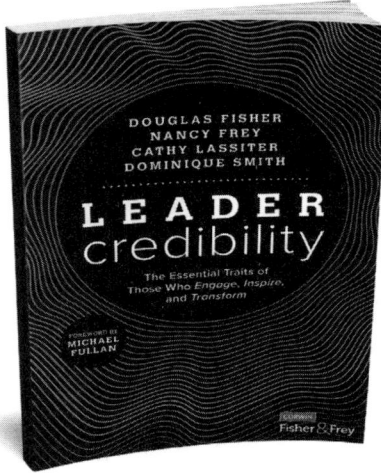